From

Date

30 devos to lighten your load

stress busters

FOR WOMEN

Freeman-Smith, LLC.
Nashville, TN 37202

The quoted ideas expressed in this book (but not Scripture verses) are not, in all cases, exact quotations, as some have been edited for clarity and brevity. In all cases, the author has attempted to maintain the speaker's original intent. In some cases, quoted material for this book was obtained from secondary sources, primarily print media. While every effort was made to ensure the accuracy of these sources, the accuracy cannot be guaranteed. For additions, deletions, corrections, or clarifications in future editions of this text, please write Freeman-Smith, LLC.

Scripture quotations are taken from:

The Holy Bible, King James Version (KJV)

The Holy Bible, New International Version (NIV) Copyright © 1973, 1978, 1984, by International Bible Society. Used by permission of Zondervan Publishing House. All rights reserved.

The Holy Bible, New King James Version (NKJV) Copyright © 1982 by Thomas Nelson, Inc. Used by permission.

Holy Bible, New Living Translation, (NLT) copyright © 1996. Used by permission of Tyndale House Publishers, Inc., Wheaton, Illinois 60189. All rights reserved.

The Message (MSG)- This edition issued by contractual arrangement with NavPress, a division of The Navigators, U.S.A. Originally published by NavPress in English as THE MESSAGE: The Bible in Contemporary Language copyright 2002-2003 by Eugene Peterson. All rights reserved.

New Century Version®. (NCV) Copyright © 1987, 1988, 1991 by Word Publishing, a division of Thomas Nelson, Inc. All rights reserved. Used by permission.

The New American Standard Bible®, (NASB) Copyright © 1960, 1962, 1963, 1968, 1971, 1972, 1973, 1975, 1977, 1995 by The Lockman Foundation. Used by permission.

The Holman Christian Standard Bible™ (HOLMAN CSB) Copyright © 1999, 2000, 2001 by Holman Bible Publishers. Used by permission.

Cover Design Kim Russell / Wahoo Designs

Page Layout by Bart Dawson

ISBN 978-1-58334-122-3

Printed in the United States of America

30 devos to lighten your load

stress
busters

FOR WOMEN

Table of Contents

Introduction

Oliver Wendell Holmes, Sr. observed, "Life is a great bundle of little things." And the same can be said for stress. Usually, we are stressed by an assortment of little things that start small but soon begin to add up. If we could simply focus on one BIG stressful event, we could probably tackle it. But life seldom works that way. Usually we have many items on our to-do lists, and each item seems to be crying out for immediate attention.

On the pages that follow, you'll be asked to spend a few minutes each day thinking about ways that you and God, working together, can organize your life, prioritize your duties, redirect your thoughts, and follow the path that your Heavenly Father intends for you to take. When you do these things, you'll receive the peace and the spiritual abundance that can, and should, be yours. So, for the next 30 days, please try this experiment: Read a chapter a day and internalize the ideas that you find here.

This text contains Biblically-based prescriptions for the inevitable challenges that accompany everyday life. As you consider your own circumstances, remember this: whatever the size of your stress, God is bigger. Much bigger. He will instruct you, protect you, energize you, and heal you if you let Him. So let Him. Pray fervently, listen carefully, work diligently, and treat every single day as an exercise in spiritual growth because that's precisely what every day can be—and will be—if you learn how to let God help you conquer stress.

Chapter 1

Beating Stress One Day at a Time

This is the day the LORD has made;
we will rejoice and be glad in it.
Psalm 118:24 NKJV

THOUGHT FOR THE DAY

Beating stress isn't a one-day achievement. To win the battle over life's everyday pressures, you'll need daily doses of perspective, perseverance, practice, and prayer.

Face facts: life can be stressful . . . very stressful. You live in a world that is brimming with demands, distractions, and deadlines (not to mention temptations, timetables, requirements, and responsibilities). Whew! No wonder you may be stressed.

What can you do in response to the stressors of everyday life? A wonderful place to start is by turning things over to God.

Psalm 118:24 reminds us that this day, like every other, is a glorious gift from the Father. How will you use that gift? Will you celebrate it and use it for His purposes? If so, you'll discover that when you turn things over to Him—when you allow God to rule over every corner of your life—He will calm your fears and guide your steps.

So today, make sure that you focus on God and upon His will for your life. Then, ask for His help. And remember: No challenge is too great for Him. Not even yours.

When in doubt, turn your worries over to God. He can handle them . . . and will.

When frustrations develop into problems that stress you out, the best way to cope is to stop, catch your breath, and do something for yourself, not out of selfishness, but out of wisdom.

Barbara Johnson

Life is strenuous. See that your clock does not run down.

Mrs. Charles E. Cowman

If you're willing to repair your life, God is willing to help. If you're not willing to repair your life, God is willing to wait.

Marie T. Freeman

God knows what each of us is dealing with. He knows our pressures. He knows our conflicts. And, He has made a provision for each and every one of them. That provision is Himself in the person of the Holy Spirit, dwelling in us and empowering us to respond rightly.

Kay Arthur

Protect Yourself Against Stress by Starting Your Day with God

He awakens [Me] each morning; He awakens My ear to listen like those being instructed. The Lord God has opened My ear, and I was not rebellious; I did not turn back.
Isaiah 50:4-5 Holman CSB

Each new day is a gift from God, and if you are wise, you will spend a few quiet moments each morning thanking the Giver. When you do, you'll discover that time spent with God can lift your spirits and relieve your stress.

Warren Wiersbe writes, "Surrender your mind to the Lord at the beginning of each day." And that's sound advice. When you begin each day with your head bowed and your heart lifted, you are reminded of God's love, His protection, and His commandments. Then, you can align your priorities for the coming day with the teachings and commandments that God has placed upon your heart.

So, if you've acquired the unfortunate habit of trying to "squeeze" God into the corners of your life, it's time to reshuffle the items on your to-do list by placing God first. And if you haven't already done so, form the habit of spending quality time with your Father in heaven. He deserves it . . . and so do you.

The manifold rewards of a serious, consistent prayer life demonstrate clearly that time with our Lord should be our first priority.

Shirley Dobson

I don't see how any Christian can survive, let alone live life as more than a conqueror, apart from a quiet time alone with God.

Kay Arthur

The Lord Jesus, available to people much of the time, left them, sometimes a great while before day, to go up to the hills where He could commune in solitude with His Father.

Elisabeth Elliot

Your habits will determine, to a surprising extent, the quality and tone of your day. In fact, daily life can be viewed as an intricate pattern woven together by the threads of habit. And no habit is more important to your spiritual health than the discipline of daily prayer and worship.

If you're serious about beating stress, then you must form the habit of talking to God first thing every morning. He's available. Are you?

A PRAYER

Heavenly Father, You never leave or forsake me.
Even when I am troubled by the demands of the day,
You are always with me, protecting me and encouraging me.
Whatever today may bring, I thank You for Your love
and Your strength. Let me lean upon You, Father,
this day and forever. Amen

NOTES TO YOURSELF ABOUT . . .

At least one step (and maybe several steps) you can
take today to relieve stress in your life.

_____

_____

_____

_____

_____

_____

_____

_____

_____

Chapter 2

Getting Enough Rest?

Come to Me, all you who labor and are heavy laden,
and I will give you rest. Take My yoke upon you and learn from Me,
for I am gentle and lowly in heart, and you will find rest
for your souls. For My yoke is easy and My burden is light.
Matthew 11:28-30 NKJV

THOUGHT FOR THE DAY

If you're not getting enough sleep, you're inviting stress into your life. You need rest, and it's up to you, and only you, to make sure you get it.

Physical exhaustion is God's way of telling us to slow down. God expects us to work hard, of course, but He also intends for us to rest. When we fail to take the rest that we need, we do a disservice to ourselves and to our families.

We live in a world that tempts us to stay up late—very late. But too much late-night TV, combined with too little sleep, is a prescription for exhaustion.

Jesus promises us that when we come to Him, He will give us rest—but we, too, must do our part. We must take the necessary steps to insure that we have sufficient rest and that we take care of our bodies in other ways, too.

As adults, each of us bears a personal responsibility for the general state of our own physical health. Certainly, various aspects of health are beyond our control: illness sometimes strikes even the healthiest men and women. But for most of us, physical health is a choice: it is the result of hundreds of small decisions that we make every day of our lives. If we make decisions that promote good health, our bodies respond. But if we fall into bad habits and undisciplined lifestyles, we suffer tragic consequences.

Are your physical or spiritual batteries running low? Is your energy on the wane? Are your emotions frayed? If so, it's time to turn your thoughts and your prayers to God's Son. And when you're finished, it's probably time to turn off the lights and go to bed!

> Your body, which is a priceless gift from God, needs a sensible amount of sleep each night. Schedule your life accordingly.

Jesus taught us by example to get out of the rat race and recharge our batteries.

Barbara Johnson

Come, come, come unto Me, Weary and sore distressed; Come, come, come unto Me, Come unto Me and rest.

Fanny Crosby

Life is strenuous. See that your clock does not run down.

Mrs. Charles E. Cowman

If we stay with the Lord, enduring to the end of His great plan for us, we will enjoy the rest that results from living in the kingdom of God.

Serita Ann Jakes

He Renews Our Strength

But those who trust in the Lord will renew their strength;
they will soar on wings like eagles;
they will run and not grow weary;
they will walk and not faint.
Isaiah 40:31 Holman CSB

When we genuinely lift our hearts and prayers to God, He renews our strength. Are you almost too stressed to lift your head? Then bow it. Offer your concerns and your fears to your Father in heaven. He is always at your side, offering His love and His strength.

Are you troubled or anxious? Take your anxieties to God in prayer. Are you weak or worried? Delve deeply into God's Holy Word and sense His presence in the quiet moments of the day. Are you spiritually exhausted? Call upon fellow believers to support you, and call upon Christ to renew your spirit and your life. Your Savior will never let you down. To the contrary, He will always lift you up if you ask Him to. So what, dear friend, are you waiting for?

He is the God of wholeness and restoration.

Stormie Omartian

Repentance removes old sins and wrong attitudes, and it opens the way for the Holy Spirit to restore our spiritual health.

Shirley Dobson

God gives us permission to forget our past and the understanding to live our present. He said He will remember our sins no more. (Psalm 103:11-12)

Serita Ann Jakes

Sometimes, we need a housecleaning of the heart.

Catherine Marshall

God can make all things new, including you. When you are weak or worried, God can renew your spirit. Your task is to let Him.

A PRAYER

Dear Lord, You have the power to make all things new.
When I grow weary, let me turn my thoughts and my prayers
to You. When I am discouraged, restore my faith in You.
Renew my strength, Father, and let me draw
comfort and courage from Your promises and from
Your unending love. Amen

NOTES TO YOURSELF ABOUT . . .

The amount of rest that you do get—and the amount of rest
that you probably should get—during
a typical 24-hour period.

Chapter 3

Pray About It

Rejoice always, pray without ceasing, in everything give thanks;
for this is the will of God in Christ Jesus for you.
1 Thessalonians 5:16-18 NKJV

THOUGHT FOR THE DAY

If you're experiencing too much stress, you should make sure that you're not neglecting your prayer life. Prayer is a powerful tool for managing stress, so pray often and early.

Want an easy-to-use, highly reliable, readily available antidote to stress? Well here it is: It's called prayer.

Is prayer an integral part of your daily life, or is it a hit-or-miss habit? Do you "pray without ceasing," or is your prayer life an afterthought? Do you regularly pray in the solitude of the early morning darkness, or do you lower your head only when others are watching? The answer to these questions will determine both the direction of your day and the way that you deal with the inevitable stressors of everyday life.

If your prayers have become more a matter of habit than a matter of passion, you're robbing yourself of a deeper relationship with God. And how can you rectify that situation? By praying more frequently and more fervently. When you do, God will shower you with His blessings, His grace, and His love.

Too many of us, even well-intentioned believers, tend to "compartmentalize" our waking hours into a few familiar categories: work, rest, play, family time, and worship. To do so is a mistake. Worship and praise should be woven into the fabric of our lives; prayer should never be relegated to a weekly three-hour visit to church on Sunday morning.

Theologian Wayne Oates once admitted, "Many of my prayers are made with my eyes open. You see, it seems I'm always praying about something, and it's not always convenient—or safe—to close my eyes." Dr. Oates understood that God always hears our prayers and that the relative position of our eyelids is of no concern to Him. So, instead of trying to do everything on your own, form the habit of asking God for His help. Begin your prayers early in the morning and continue them throughout the day. And remember this: God does answer your prayers, but He's not likely to answer those prayers until you've prayed them.

If you find yourself becoming overly stressed, find a quiet place to go and pray. Ask God for His guidance, and while you're at it, ask Him to give you the courage to meet the challenges ahead. And rest assured: When you ask, He answers.

What God gives in answer to our prayers will always be the thing we most urgently need, and it will always be sufficient.

Elisabeth Elliot

When the Holy Spirit comes to dwell within us, I believe we gain a built-in inclination to take our concerns and needs to the Lord in prayer.

Shirley Dobson

Ask God for Help

Now if any of you lacks wisdom,
he should ask God, who gives to all generously
and without criticizing, and it will be given to him.
James 1:5 Holman CSB

Sometimes, amid the stresses and the frustrations of daily life, we forget to slow ourselves down long enough to talk with God. Instead of turning our thoughts and prayers to Him, we rely entirely upon our own resources, with decidedly mixed results. Or, instead of praying for strength, we seek to manufacture it within ourselves, only to find that lasting strength remains elusive.

Are you in need? Ask God to sustain you. And while you're in the mood to ask, don't be afraid to ask for the loving support of your family and friends. When you ask for help, you're likely to receive it. But if you're unwilling to ask, why should you expect to receive it?

So the next time times get tough, remember that help is on the way . . . all you must do is ask.

God will help us become the people we are meant to be, if only we will ask Him.

Hannah Whitall Smith

Often I have made a request of God with earnest pleadings even backed up with Scripture, only to have Him say "No" because He had something better in store.

Ruth Bell Graham

When will we realize that we're not troubling God with our questions and concerns? His heart is open to hear us—his touch nearer than our next thought—as if no one in the world existed but us. Our very personal God wants to hear from us personally.

Gigi Graham Tchividjian

If you want more from life, ask more from God. If you're searching for peace and abundance, ask for God's help—and keep asking—until He answers your prayers. If you sincerely want to rise above the stresses and complications of everyday life, ask for God's help many times each day.

A PRAYER

Dear Lord, make me a person whose constant prayers are pleasing to You. Let me come to You often with concerns both great and small. And, when You answer my prayers, Father, let me trust Your answers, today and forever. Amen

NOTES TO YOURSELF ABOUT . . .
The role that prayer does play—and the role that it should play—in your everyday life.

Chapter 4

The Direction
of Your Thoughts

Guard your heart above all else, for it is the source of life.
Proverbs 4:23 Holman CSB

THOUGHT FOR THE DAY

Since your thoughts have the power to increase the amount
of stress you feel—or eliminate stress altogether—you should be
careful to monitor the quality, the direction, and the veracity
of those thoughts.

The level of stress you experience is determined, to a surprising extent, by the direction of your thoughts. If you focus your thoughts and energies on matters that honor your God, your family, and yourself, you will reap rich rewards. But if you focus too intently on the distractions and temptations of our 21st-century world, you're inviting large quantities of trouble.

What is your focus today? Are you willing to focus your thoughts and energies on God's blessings and upon His will for your life? Or will you turn your thoughts to other things? Before you answer that question, consider this: God created you in His own image, and He wants you to experience joy and abundance. But, God will not force His joy upon you; you must claim it for yourself.

Today, why not focus your thoughts on the joy that is rightfully yours in Christ? Why not take time to celebrate God's glorious creation? Why not trust your hopes instead of your fears? Focus, not on the world's priorities, but on God's priorities. When you do, you'll experience the peace and the power that accrues to those who put Jesus first in their lives.

It is the thoughts and intents of the heart that shape a person's life.

John Eldredge

Watch what you think. If your inner voice is, in reality, your inner critic, you need to tone down the criticism now. And while you're at it, train yourself to begin thinking thoughts that are more rational, more accepting, and less judgmental.

As we have by faith said no to sin, so we should by faith say yes to God and set our minds on things above, where Christ is seated in the heavenlies.

Vonette Bright

No more imperfect thoughts. No more sad memories. No more ignorance. My redeemed body will have a redeemed mind. Grant me a foretaste of that perfect mind as you mirror your thoughts in me today.

Joni Eareckson Tada

The things we think are the things that feed our souls. If we think on pure and lovely things, we shall grow pure and lovely like them; and the converse is equally true.

Hannah Whitall Smith

Perspective for Today

*Don't abandon wisdom, and she will watch over you;
love her, and she will guard you.*
Proverbs 4:6 Holman CSB

Sometimes, amid the demands of daily life, we lose perspective. Life seems out of balance, and the pressures of everyday living seem overwhelming. What's needed is a fresh perspective, a restored sense of balance . . . and God.

If a temporary loss of perspective has left you worried, exhausted, or both, it's time to readjust your thought patterns. Negative thoughts are habit-forming; thankfully, so are positive ones. With practice, you can form the habit of focusing on God's priorities and your possibilities. When you do, you'll soon discover that you will spend less time fretting about your challenges and more time praising God for His gifts.

When you call upon the Lord and prayerfully seek His will, He will give you wisdom and perspective. When you make God's priorities your priorities, He will direct your steps and calm your fears. So today and every day hereafter, pray for a sense of balance and perspective. And remember: your thoughts are intensely powerful things, so handle them with care.

Like a shadow declining swiftly . . . away . . . like the dew of the morning gone with the heat of the day; like the wind in the treetops, like a wave of the sea, so are our lives on earth when seen in light of eternity.

Ruth Bell Graham

The proper perspective creates within us a spirit of reaching outside of ourselves with joy and enthusiasm.

Luci Swindoll

Instead of being frustrated and overwhelmed by all that is going on in our world, go to the Lord and ask Him to give you His eternal perspective.

Kay Arthur

Attitude is the mind's paintbrush; it can color any situation.

Barbara Johnson

Remember that your life is an integral part of God's grand plan. So don't become unduly upset over the minor inconveniences, and don't worry too much about today's setbacks—they're temporary.

A PRAYER

Dear Lord, when the pace of my life becomes frantic, slow
me down and give me perspective. Give me the wisdom to
realize that the problems of today are only temporary but
that Your love is eternal. When I become discouraged, keep
me steady and sure, so that I might do Your will here on
earth and then live with You forever in heaven. Amen

NOTES TO YOURSELF ABOUT . . .
Better ways that you can think about the issues
that are stressing you.

_____

_____

_____

_____

_____

_____

_____

_____

_____

_____

Chapter 5

The Right Priorities

Let us walk with decency, as in the daylight:
not in carousing and drunkenness.
Romans 13:13 Holman CSB

THOUGHT FOR THE DAY

Since you can't do everything, you must set priorities. So make sure that your priorities are appropriate to your circumstances and pleasing to God.

On your daily to-do list, all items are not created equal: Certain tasks are extremely important while others are not. Therefore, it's imperative that you prioritize your daily activities and complete each task in the approximate order of its importance.

The principle of doing first things first is simple in theory but more complicated in practice. Well-meaning family, friends, and coworkers have a way of making unexpected demands upon your time. Furthermore, each day has it own share of minor emergencies; these urgent matters tend to draw your attention away from more important ones. On paper, prioritizing is simple, but to act upon those priorities in the real world requires maturity, patience, determination, and balance.

If you fail to prioritize your day, life will automatically do the job for you. So your choice is simple: prioritize or be prioritized. It's a choice that will help determine the quality of your life.

If you're having trouble balancing the many demands of everyday living, perhaps you've been trying to organize your life according to your own plans, not God's. A better strategy, of course, is to take your daily obligations and place them in the hands of the One who created you. To do so, you must prioritize your day according to God's commandments, and you must seek His will and His wisdom in all matters. Then, you can face the coming day with the assurance that the same God who created our universe out of nothingness will help you place first things first in your own life.

Are you living a balanced life that allows time for worship, for family, for work, for exercise, and a little time left over for you? Or do you feel overworked, under-appreciated, overwhelmed, and underpaid? If your to-do list is "maxed out" and your energy is on the wane, it's time to restore a sense of balance to your life. You can do so by turning the concerns and the priorities of this day over to God—prayerfully, earnestly, and often. Then, you must listen for His answer . . . and trust the answer He gives.

As you're prioritizing your day, ask God to help you sort out big responsibilities from small ones, major problems from minor ones, and important responsibilities from irrelevant ones. And when you're faced with a big decision, let God help you decide.

There were endless demands on Jesus' time. Still he was able to make that amazing claim of "completing the work you gave me to do." (John 17:4 NIV)

Elisabeth Elliot

Have you prayed about your resources lately? Find out how God wants you to use your time and your money. No matter what it costs, forsake all that is not of God.

Kay Arthur

Managing Time Wisely

Teach us to number our days carefully so that we may develop wisdom in our hearts.
Psalm 90:12 Holman CSB

Time is a nonrenewable gift from God. But sometimes, we treat our time here on earth as if it were not a gift at all: We may be tempted to invest our lives in trivial pursuits and petty diversions. But our Father beckons each of us to a higher calling.

An important element of our stewardship to God is the way that we choose to spend the time He has entrusted to us. Each waking moment holds the potential to do a good deed, to say a kind word, or to offer a heartfelt prayer. Our challenge, as believers, is to use our time wisely in the service of God's work and in accordance with His plan for our lives.

Each day is a special treasure to be savored and celebrated. May we—as Christians who have so much to celebrate—never fail to praise our Creator by rejoicing in this glorious day, and by using it wisely.

Frustration is not the will of God. There is time to do anything and everything that God wants us to do.

Elisabeth Elliot

God has a present will for your life. It is neither chaotic nor utterly exhausting. In the midst of many good choices vying for your time, He will give you the discernment to recognize what is best.

Beth Moore

Our time is short! The time we can invest for God, in creative things, in receiving our fellowmen for Christ, is short!

Billy Graham

The best use of life is love. The best expression of love is time. The best time to love is now.

Rick Warren

Feeling overwhelmed? Perhaps you're not doing a very good job of setting priorities—or perhaps you're allowing other people to set your priorities for you. In either case, perhaps it's time for a change.

A PRAYER

Dear Lord, You have given me a wonderful gift:
time here on earth. Let me use it wisely—for the glory
of Your kingdom and the betterment of Your world—
today and every day. Amen

NOTES TO YOURSELF ABOUT . . .

Better strategies for organizing your day and your life.

_____

_____

_____

_____

_____

_____

_____

_____

_____

_____

Chapter 6

Saying Yes to God

Cast your burden on the Lord, and He will support you;
He will never allow the righteous to be shaken.
Psalm 55:22 Holman CSB

THOUGHT FOR THE DAY

When you say "yes" to God, you won't eliminate all stressors from your life, but you will receive His blessings today and throughout eternity.

Your decision to seek a deeper relationship with God will not remove all problems from your life; to the contrary, it will bring about a series of personal crises as you constantly seek to say "yes" to God although the world encourages you to do otherwise. You live in a world that seeks to snare your attention and lead you away from God. Each time you are tempted to distance yourself from the Creator, you will face a spiritual crisis. A few of these crises may be monumental in scope, but most will be the small, everyday decisions of life. In fact, life here on earth can be seen as one test after another—and with each crisis comes yet another opportunity to grow closer to God . . . or to distance yourself from His plan for your life.

Today, you will face many opportunities to say "yes" to your Creator—and you will also encounter many opportunities to say "no" to Him. Your answers will determine the quality of your day and the direction of your life, so answer carefully . . . very carefully.

If you're facing a crisis, don't face it alone. Enlist God's help. And then, when you've finished praying about your problem, don't be afraid to seek help from family, from friends, or from your pastor.

We all go through pain and sorrow, but the presence of God, like a warm, comforting blanket, can shield us and protect us, and allow the deep inner joy to surface, even in the most devastating circumstances.

Barbara Johnson

When considering the size of your problems, there are two categories that you should never worry about: the problems that are small enough for you to handle, and the ones that aren't too big for God to handle.

Marie T. Freeman

Often the trials we mourn are really gateways into the good things we long for.

Hannah Whitall Smith

Recently I've been learning that life comes down to this: God is in everything. Regardless of what difficulties I am experiencing at the moment, or what things aren't as I would like them to be, I look at the circumstances and say, "Lord, what are you trying to teach me?"

Catherine Marshall

Good Decisions Mean Less Stress

But Daniel purposed in his heart that he
would not defile himself . . . .
Daniel 1:8 KJV

Life presents each of us with countless questions, conundrums, doubts, and problems. Thankfully, the riddles of everyday living are not too difficult to solve if we look for answers in the right places. When we have questions, we should consult God's Word, we should consult our own consciences, and we should consult a few close friends and family members.

Perhaps Søren Kierkegaard was stating the obvious when he observed, "Life can only be understood backwards; but it must be lived forwards." Still, Kierkegaard's words are far easier to understand than they are to live by.

Taking a forward-looking (and stress-conquering) approach to life means learning the art of solving difficult problems sensibly and consistently . . . and sooner rather than later.

When we learn to listen to Christ's voice for the details of our daily decisions, we begin to know Him personally.

Catherine Marshall

The Reference Point for the Christian is the Bible. All values, judgments, and attitudes must be gauged in relationship to this Reference Point.

Ruth Bell Graham

There may be no trumpet sound or loud applause when we make a right decision, just a calm sense of resolution and peace.

Gloria Gaither

Good and evil both increase at compound interest. That is why the little decisions you and I make every day are of such infinite importance.

C. S. Lewis

Never take on a major obligation of any kind without first taking sufficient time to carefully consider whether or not you should commit to it. The bigger the obligation, the more days you should take to decide. If someone presses you for an answer before you are ready, your automatic answer should always be "No."

A PRAYER

Dear Lord, when life seems chaotic, remind me of Your love
and protection. Difficult times provide opportunities
for me to grow closer to You. Thank You for all that
this day has to offer. Amen

NOTES TO YOURSELF ABOUT . . .

One decision you can make today that will reduce stress
and improve your life.

_____

_____

_____

_____

_____

_____

_____

_____

_____

Chapter 7

God Can Handle It

I will lift up my eyes to the hills. From whence comes my help?
My help comes from the Lord, Who made heaven and earth.

Psalm 121:1-2 NKJV

THOUGHT FOR THE DAY

God is big enough and strong enough to solve any problem
you will ever face.

Stressful days are an inevitable fact of modern life. And how do we best cope with the challenges of our demanding, 21st-century world? By turning our days and our lives over to God. Elisabeth Elliot writes, "If my life is surrendered to God, all is well. Let me not grab it back, as though it were in peril in His hand but would be safer in mine!" Yet even the most devout Christian woman may, at times, seek to grab the reins of her life and proclaim, "I'm in charge!" To do so is foolish, prideful, and stressful.

When we seek to impose our own wills upon the world—or upon other people—we invite stress into our lives . . . needlessly. But, when we turn our lives and our hearts over to God—when we accept His will instead of seeking vainly to impose our own—we discover the inner peace that can be ours through Him.

Do you feel overwhelmed by the stresses of daily life? Turn your concerns and your prayers over to God. Trust Him. Trust Him completely. Trust Him today. Trust Him always. When it comes to the inevitable challenges of this day, hand them over to God completely and without reservation. He knows your needs and will meet those needs in His own way and in His own time if you let Him.

God is God whether we recognize it or not. Nothing about that can change, except us.

Lisa Whelchel

Remember that God can handle your problems. Bill Hybels writes, "Pour out your heart to God and tell Him how you feel. Be real, be honest, and when you get it all out, you'll start to feel the gradual covering of God's comforting presence." Enough said.

Either we are adrift in chaos or we are individuals, created, loved, upheld, and placed purposefully, exactly where we are. Can you believe that? Can you trust God for that?

Elisabeth Elliot

God is in control, and therefore in everything I can give thanks, not because of the situation, but because of the One who directs and rules over it.

Kay Arthur

The choice for me is to either look at all things I have lost or the things I have. To live in fear or to live in hope. Hope comes from knowing I have a sovereign, loving God who is in every event in my life.

Lisa Beamer (Her husband Todd was killed on flight 93, 9-11-01)

Rely upon Him

Humble yourselves therefore under the mighty hand of God,
so that He may exalt you in due time,
casting all your care upon Him,
because He cares about you.
1 Peter 5:6-7 Holman CSB

Do the stresses of this day threaten to overwhelm you? If so, you must rely not only upon your own resources but also upon the promises of your Father in heaven.

God is a never-ending source of support and courage for those of us who call upon Him. When we are weary, He gives us strength. When we see no hope, God reminds us of His promises. When we grieve, God wipes away our tears.

God will hold your hand and walk with you every day of your life if you let Him. So even if your circumstances are difficult, trust the Father. His love is eternal and His goodness endures forever.

Our hearts are prone to wander and tempted to squander our Father's inheritance on the world's cheap amusements. But, when our eyes awaken to reality, when we lift our heads above the compromise, and when our stomachs ache for the food of home, a certain Father will always be standing at the gate, ready to prepare a feast for us, waiting anxiously for His prodigal to come home.

Beth Moore

Make the least of all that goes and the most of all that comes. Don't regret what is past. Cherish what you have. Look forward to all that is to come. And most important of all, rely moment by moment on Jesus Christ.

Gigi Graham Tchividjian

God walks with us. He scoops us up in His arms or simply sits with us in silent strength until we cannot avoid the awesome recognition that yes, even now, He is here.

Gloria Gaither

Today, think about ways that you can tap into God's strength. Try prayer, worship, and praise, for starters.

A PRAYER

Dear Lord, whatever "it" is, You can handle it!
Let me turn to You when I am fearful or worried.
You are my loving Father, and I will always trust You. Amen

NOTES TO YOURSELF ABOUT . . .

God's love for you and His promise to protect you today,
tomorrow, and forever.

_____

_____

_____

_____

_____

_____

_____

_____

_____

_____

Chapter 8

Learning the Art of Acceptance

Come to terms with God and be at peace;
in this way good will come to you.
Job 22:21 Holman CSB

THOUGHT FOR THE DAY

It's important to do your best and trust God with the rest. And that means accepting the things you cannot change.

Sometimes, we must accept life on its terms, not our own. Life has a way of unfolding, not as we will, but as it will. And sometimes, there is precious little we can do to change things. When events transpire that are beyond our control, we have a choice: we can either learn the art of acceptance, or we can make ourselves miserable as we struggle to change the unchangeable.

The American theologian Reinhold Niebuhr composed a profoundly simple verse that came to be known as the Serenity Prayer:

"God, grant me the serenity to accept the things I cannot change, the courage to change the things I can, and the wisdom to know the difference."

Niebuhr's words are far easier to recite than they are to live by. Why? Because most of us want life to unfold in accordance with our own wishes and timetables. But sometimes God has other plans.

Author Hannah Whitall Smith observed, "How changed our lives would be if we could only fly through the days on wings of surrender and trust!" These words remind us that even when we cannot understand the workings of God, we must trust Him and accept His will. So if you've encountered unfortunate circumstances that are beyond your power to control, accept those circumstances . . . and trust God. When you do, you can be comforted in the knowledge that your Creator is both loving and wise, and that He understands His plans perfectly, even when you do not.

Acceptance means learning to trust God more. Today, think of at least one aspect of your life that you've been reluctant to accept, and then prayerfully ask God to help you trust Him more by accepting the past.

He does not need to transplant us into a different field. He transforms the very things that were before our greatest hindrances, into the chief and most blessed means of our growth. No difficulties in your case can baffle Him. Put yourself absolutely into His hands, and let Him have His own way with you.

Elisabeth Elliot

Ultimately things work out best for those who make the best of the way things work out.

Barbara Johnson

Making Peace with Your Past

Do not remember the past events, pay no attention to things of old.
Look, I am about to do something new; even now it is coming.
Do you not see it? Indeed, I will make a way
in the wilderness, rivers in the desert.
Isaiah 43:18-19 Holman CSB

Because you are human, you may be slow to forget yesterday's disappointments. But, if you sincerely seek to focus your hopes and energies on the future, then you must find ways to accept the past, no matter how difficult it may be to do so.

Have you made peace with your past? If so, congratulations. But, if you are mired in the quicksand of regret, it's time to plan your escape. How can you do so? By accepting what has been and by trusting God for what will be.

So, if you have not yet made peace with the past, today is the day to declare an end to all hostilities. When you do, you can then turn your thoughts to wondrous promises of God and to the glorious future that He has in store for you.

When we do what is right, we have contentment, peace, and happiness.

Beverly LaHaye

To know God as He really is—in His essential nature and character—is to arrive at a citadel of peace that circumstances may storm, but can never capture.

Catherine Marshall

In the center of a hurricane there is absolute quiet and peace. There is no safer place than in the center of the will of God.

Corrie ten Boom

I believe that in every time and place it is within our power to acquiesce in the will of God—and what peace it brings to do so!

Elisabeth Elliot

The past is past, so don't live there. If you're focused on the past, change your focus. If you're living in the past, it's time to stop living there.

A PRAYER

Father, the events of this world unfold according to a plan
that I cannot fully understand. But You understand.
Help me to trust You, Lord, even when I am grieving.
Help me to trust You even when I am confused. Today,
in whatever circumstances I find myself, let me trust
Your will and accept Your love . . . completely. Amen

NOTES TO YOURSELF ABOUT . . .

Painful episodes in your past that you must learn to accept.

_____

_____

_____

_____

_____

_____

_____

_____

_____

_____

Chapter 9

Out of Balance?

Then the apostles gathered to Jesus and told Him all things, both what they had done and what they had taught. And He said to them, "Come aside by yourselves to a deserted place and rest a while." For there were many coming and going, and they did not even have time to eat.

Mark 6:30-31 NKJV

THOUGHT FOR THE DAY

Unless you can learn to balance your obligations and choose only the most important tasks, you'll find yourself overworked, under-appreciated, and stressed out. So your challenge is straightforward: to find the appropriate balance between family, work, fun, rest, exercise, and God.

Face facts: life is a delicate balancing act, a tightrope walk with over-commitment on one side and under-commitment on the other. And it's up to each of us to walk carefully on that rope, not falling prey to pride (which causes us to attempt too much) or to fear (which causes us to attempt too little).

God's Word promises us the possibility of abundance (John 10:10). And we are far more likely to experience that abundance when we lead balanced lives.

When you allow yourself to take on too many jobs, you simply can't do all of them well. That means that if you allow yourself to become overcommitted, whether at home, at work, at church, or anywhere in between, you're asking for trouble. So you must learn how to say no to the things you don't have the time or the energy to do.

Of course, sometimes, saying no can be tough. Why? Because well-meaning women (like you) genuinely want to help other people out. But if you allow yourself to become overworked, you may begin over-promising and under-serving—and you'll disappoint just about everybody, including yourself.

It is important that we take time out for ourselves—for relaxation, for refreshment.

Ruth Bell Graham

Strive for balance. Lots of people are clamoring for your attention, your time, and your energy. It's up to you to establish priorities that are important for you and your family. And remember, if you don't establish priorities, the world has a way of doing the job for you.

The balance of affirmation and discipline, freedom and restraint, encouragement and warning is different for each child and season and generation, yet the absolutes of God's Word are necessary and trustworthy no matter how mercuric the time.

Gloria Gaither

A balanced woman of God sees herself as valuable, gifted, responsible for her own growth and maturity—not overly dependent on anyone to get her through life or to make her secure.

Charles Swindoll

When I feel like circumstances are spiraling downward in my life, God taught me that whether I'm right side up or upside down, I need to turn those circumstances over to Him. He is the only one who can bring balance into my life.

Carole Lewis

Too Busy?

The plans of the diligent certainly lead to profit,
but anyone who is reckless only becomes poor.
Proverbs 21:5 Holman CSB

Has the hectic pace of life robbed you of the peace that might otherwise be yours through Jesus Christ? Are you one of those people who is simply too busy for your own good? If so, you're doing everybody a disservice by heaping needless stresses upon yourself and your loved ones.

God offers you a peace that passes human understanding, but He won't force His peace upon you; in order to experience it, you must slow down long enough to sense His presence and His love.

Today, as a gift to yourself, to your family, and to your world, invite Christ to preside over every aspect of your life. It's the best way to live and the surest path to peace . . . today and forever.

In our tense, uptight society where folks are rushing to make appointments they have already missed, a good laugh can be as refreshing as a cup of cold water in the desert.

Barbara Johnson

If you can't seem to find time for God, then you're simply too busy for your own good. God is never too busy for you, and you should never be too busy for Him.

Marie T. Freeman

Being busy, in and of itself, is not a sin. But being busy in an endless pursuit of things that leave us empty and hollow and broken inside—that cannot be pleasing to God.

Max Lucado

We often become mentally and spiritually barren because we're so busy.

Franklin Graham

Too busy? Try to do first things first, and keep your focus on high-priority tasks. And remember this: your highest priority should be your relationship with God and His Son.

A PRAYER

Father, let me find contentment and balance.
Let Your priorities be my priorities, and when
I have done my best, give me the wisdom to place
my faith and my trust in You. Amen

NOTES TO YOURSELF ABOUT . . .

Three things you can do to bring more balance to your life.

_____

_____

_____

_____

_____

_____

_____

_____

_____

_____

Chapter 10

Defeating Procrastination

Now, Lord, what do I wait for? My hope is in You.
Psalm 39:7 Holman CSB

THOUGHT FOR THE DAY

Procrastination increases stress; intelligent action decreases it. Act accordingly.

Procrastination and stress are traveling companions. So it's up to you to figure out how to defeat procrastination before it defeats you.

If you find yourself bound by the chains of procrastination, ask yourself what you're waiting for—or more accurately what you're afraid of—and why. As you examine the emotional roadblocks that have, heretofore, blocked your path, you may discover that you're waiting for the "perfect" moment, that instant in time when you feel neither afraid nor anxious. But in truth, perfect moments like these are few and far between.

So stop waiting for the perfect moment and focus, instead, on finding the right moment to do what needs to be done. Then, trust God and get busy. When you do, you'll discover that you and the Father, working together, can accomplish great things . . . and that you can accomplish them sooner rather than later.

Once you acquire the habit of doing what needs to be done when it needs to be done, you will avoid untold trouble, worry, and stress. So learn to overcome procrastination by paying less attention to your fears and more attention to your responsibilities. God has created a world that punishes procrastinators and rewards people who "do it now." In other words, life doesn't procrastinate. Neither should you.

It's easy to put off unpleasant tasks until "later." A far better strategy is this: Do the unpleasant work first so you can enjoy the rest of the day.

Never fail to do something because you don't feel like it. Sometimes you just have to do it now, and you'll feel like it later.

Marie T. Freeman

From the very moment one feels called to act is born the strength to bear whatever horror one will feel or see. In some inexplicable way, terror loses its overwhelming power when it becomes a task that must be faced.

Emmi Bonhoeffer

Not now becomes never.

Martin Luther

We spend our lives dreaming of the future, not realizing that a little of it slips away every day.

Barbara Johnson

Facing Fears

Do not fear, for I am with you; do not be afraid,
for I am your God. I will strengthen you; I will help you;
I will hold on to you with My righteous right hand.
Isaiah 41:10 Holman CSB

We live in a world that is, at times, a frightening place. We live in a world that is, at times, a discouraging place. We live in a world where life-changing losses can be so painful and so profound that it seems we will never recover. But, with God's help, and with the help of encouraging family members and friends, we can recover.

During the darker days of life, we are wise to remember the words of Jesus, who reassured His disciples, saying, "Take courage! It is I. Don't be afraid" (Matthew 14:27 NIV). Then, with God's comfort and His love in our hearts, we can offer encouragement to others. And by helping them face their fears, we can, in turn, tackle our own problems with courage, determination, and faith.

If a person fears God, he or she has no reason to fear anything else. On the other hand, if a person does not fear God, then fear becomes a way of life.

Beth Moore

Fear knocked at the door. Faith answered. No one was there.

Anonymous

Worry is a cycle of inefficient thoughts whirling around a center of fear.

Corrie ten Boom

When once we are assured that God is good, then there can be nothing left to fear.

Hannah Whitall Smith

If you're feeling fearful, anxious, or stressed, you must trust God to solve the problems that are simply too big for you to solve.

A PRAYER

Dear Lord, today is a new day. Help me tackle
the important tasks immediately, even if those tasks
are unpleasant. Don't let me put off until tomorrow
what I should do today. Amen

NOTES TO YOURSELF ABOUT . . .

An important task that you've been putting off . . . and how
your life might be improved if you overcame procrastination.

_____

_____

_____

_____

_____

_____

_____

_____

_____

_____

Chapter 11

Your Own Worst Critic?

For You formed my inward parts; You covered me in my mother's womb. I will praise You, for I am fearfully and wonderfully made; Marvelous are Your works.
Psalm 139:13-14 NKJV

THOUGHT FOR THE DAY

If you become your own worst critic, you're creating needless stress for yourself and your loved ones.

Are you your own worst critic? And in response to that criticism, are you constantly trying to transform yourself into a person who meets society's expectations, but not God's expectations? If so, it's time to become a little more understanding of the person you see whenever you look into the mirror.

Being patient with other people can be difficult. But sometimes, we find it even more difficult to be patient with ourselves. We have high expectations and lofty goals. We want to receive God's blessings now, not later. And, of course, we want our lives to unfold according to our own wishes and our own timetables—not God's. Yet throughout the Bible, we are instructed that patience is the companion of wisdom. Proverbs 16:32 teaches us that "Patience is better than strength" (NCV). God's message, then, is clear: we must be patient with all people—including ourselves.

The Bible affirms the importance of self-acceptance by exhorting believers to love others as they love themselves (Matthew 22:37-40). Furthermore, the Bible teaches that when we genuinely open our hearts to Him, God accepts us just as we are. And, if He accepts us—faults and all—then who are we to believe otherwise?

If you find yourself focussing too much on your appearance, it's time to find a different focus. Remember that God sees you as you really are, and it's God's view that matters.

If you can forgive the person you were, accept the person you are, and believe in the person you will become, you are headed for joy. So celebrate your life.

Barbara Johnson

I can promise you that until you learn that solitude is your friend and not your enemy, until you are comfortable "staying in your own orbit," you will have little to give anyone else.

Luci Swindoll

Being loved by Him whose opinion matters most gives us the security to risk loving, too—even loving ourselves.

Gloria Gaither

As you and I lay up for ourselves living, lasting treasures in Heaven, we come to the awesome conclusion that we ourselves are His treasure!

Anne Graham Lotz

Defeating Negativity

A person with great anger bears the penalty;
if you rescue him, you'll have to do it again.
Proverbs 19:19 Holman CSB

From experience, we know that it is easy to criticize others. And we know that it is usually far easier to find faults than to find solutions. Still, the urge to criticize others remains a powerful temptation for most of us.

Negativity is highly contagious: We give it to others who, in turn, give it back to us. This stress-inducing cycle can be broken only by positive thoughts, heartfelt prayers, encouraging words, and meaningful acts of kindness.

As thoughtful servants of a loving God, we have no valid reason—and no legitimate excuse—to be negative. So, when we are tempted to be overly critical of others, or unfairly critical of ourselves, we must use the transforming power of God's love to break the chains of negativity. We must defeat negativity before negativity defeats us.

Winners see an answer for every problem; losers see a problem in every answer.

Barbara Johnson

We never get anywhere—nor do our conditions and circumstances change—when we look at the dark side of life.

Mrs. Charles E. Cowman

After one hour in heaven, we shall be ashamed that we ever grumbled.

Vance Havner

When we get rid of inner conflicts and wrong attitudes toward life, we will almost automatically burst into joy.

E. Stanley Jones

Negative thinking breeds more negative thinking, so nip negativity in the bud, starting today and continuing every day of your life.

A PRAYER

Lord, I have so much to learn and so many ways to improve
myself, but You love me just as I am. Thank You for
Your love and for Your Son. And, help me to become
the person that You want me to become. Amen

NOTES TO YOURSELF ABOUT . . .

The need to forgive yourself (and others)
for mistakes and imperfections.

Chapter 12

Keeping Up with the Joneses?

For where your treasure is, there your heart will be also.
Luke 12:34 Holman CSB

THOUGHT FOR THE DAY

For children and adults alike, peer pressure can be very stressful. Your job, therefore, is to worry more about pleasing God and less about pleasing your friends or neighbors.

As a member-in-good-standing in this highly competitive, 21st-century world, you know that the demands and expectations of everyday living can seem burdensome, even overwhelming at times. Keeping up with the Joneses can become a stress-inducing, ego-deflating, 24-hour-a-day job if you let it. A better strategy, of course, is to stop trying to please the neighbors and to concentrate, instead, on pleasing God.

Perhaps you have set your goals high; if so, congratulations! You're willing to dream big dreams, and that's a very good thing. But as you consider your life's purpose, don't allow your quest for excellence to interfere with the spiritual journey that God has planned for you.

As a Christian, your instructions are clear: you must try to please God first and always. And how do you please Him? By accepting His Son and by obeying His commandments. All other concerns—including, but not limited to, keeping up appearances—are of relatively little importance. So if you're making purchases in order to impress the Joneses—or anybody else, for that matter—stop it! Pleasing God (by leading a sensible, moderate life that gives you time and energy to focus on Him) is more important than impressing your neighbors . . . far more important.

You will get untold flak for prioritizing God's revealed and present will for your life over man's . . . but, boy, is it worth it.

Beth Moore

If you find yourself focusing too much on stuff, try spending a little less time at the mall and a little more time talking to God. And remember this fact: Too much stuff doesn't eliminate stress. In fact, having too much stuff can actually create stress.

For better or worse, you will eventually become more and more like the people you associate with. So why not associate with people who make you better, not worse?

Marie T. Freeman

Ambition! We must be careful what we mean by it. If it means the desire to get ahead of other people—which is what I think it does mean—then it is bad. If it simply means wanting to do a thing well, then it is good. It isn't wrong for an actor to want to act his part as well as it can possibly be acted, but the wish to have his name in bigger type than the other actors is a bad one.

C. S. Lewis

We, as God's people, are not only to stay far away from sin and sinners who would entice us, but we are to be so like our God that we mourn over sin.

Kay Arthur

Beyond Envy

*Therefore, laying aside all malice, all deceit, hypocrisy, envy,
and all evil speaking, as newborn babes,
desire the pure milk of the word, that you may grow thereby.*
1 Peter 2:1-2 NKJV

Because we are frail, imperfect human beings, we are sometimes envious of others. But God's Word warns us that envy is sin. Thus, we must guard ourselves against the natural tendency to feel resentment and jealousy when other people experience good fortune. As believers, we have absolutely no reason to be envious of any people on earth. After all, as Christians we are already recipients of the greatest gift in all creation: God's grace. We have been promised the gift of eternal life through God's only begotten Son, and we must count that gift as our most precious possession.

So here's a simple suggestion that is guaranteed to reduce stress and increase happiness: fill your heart with God's love, God's promises, and God's Son . . . and when you do so, leave no room for envy, hatred, bitterness, or regret.

Contentment comes when we develop an attitude of gratitude for the important things we do have in our lives that we tend to take for granted if we have our eyes staring longingly at our neighbor's stuff.

Dave Ramsey

Is there somebody who's always getting your goat? Talk to the Shepherd.

Anonymous

What God asks, does, or requires of others is not my business; it is His.

Kay Arthur

Discontent dries up the soul.

Elisabeth Elliot

Envy is a sin, a sin that robs you of contentment and increases stress. So you must steadfastly refuse to let feelings of envy invade your thoughts or your heart.

A PRAYER

Dear Lord, other people may encourage me to stray from
Your path, but I wish to follow in the footsteps of Your Son.
Give me the vision to see the right path—and the wisdom to
follow it—today and every day of my life. Amen

NOTES TO YOURSELF ABOUT . . .

The dangers (and stresses) of trying to keep up
with the Joneses.

_____

_____

_____

_____

_____

_____

_____

_____

_____

_____

Chapter 13

In Times of Adversity

For whatever is born of God overcomes the world.
And this is the victory that has overcome the world—our faith.
1 John 5:4 NKJV

THOUGHT FOR THE DAY

When tough times arrive, you should work as if everything
depended upon you and pray as if everything depended upon
God.

As life here on earth unfolds, all of us encounter occasional stresses and setbacks: Those occasional visits from Old Man Trouble are simply a fact of life, and none of us are exempt. When tough times arrive, we may be forced to rearrange our plans and our priorities. But even on our darkest days, we must remember that God's love remains constant.

The fact that we encounter adversity is not nearly so important as the way we choose to deal with it. We have a clear choice: we can either begin the difficult work of tackling our troubles . . . or not. When we summon the courage to look Old Man Trouble squarely in the eye, he usually blinks. But, if we refuse to address our problems, even the smallest stresses have a way of growing into king-sized catastrophes.

Psalm 145 promises, "The Lord is near to all who call on him, to all who call on him in truth. He fulfills the desires of those who fear him; he hears their cry and saves them" (vv. 18-20 NIV). And the words of Jesus offer us comfort: "These things I have spoken to you, that in Me you may have peace. In the world you will have tribulation; but be of good cheer, I have overcome the world" (John 16:33 NKJV).

As believers, we know that God loves us and that He will protect us. In times of hardship, He will comfort us; in times of sorrow, He will dry our tears. When we are troubled or weak or sorrowful, God is always with us. We must build our lives on the rock that cannot be shaken: we must trust in God. And then, we must get on with the hard work of tackling our problems . . . because if we don't, who will? Or should?

If you're having tough times, don't hit the panic button and don't keep everything bottled up inside. Talk things over with your family or your spouse, and if necessary, find a counselor you can really trust. A second opinion (or, for that matter, a third, fourth, or fifth opinion) is usually helpful. So if your troubles seem overwhelming, be willing to seek outside help.

Every misfortune, every failure, every loss may be transformed. God has the power to transform all misfortunes into "God-sends."

Mrs. Charles E. Cowman

Are you weak? Weary? Confused? Troubled? Pressured? How is your relationship with God? Is it held in its place of priority? I believe the greater the pressure, the greater your need for time alone with Him.

Kay Arthur

Confidence Restored

I have told you these things so that in Me you may have peace.
In the world you have suffering. But take courage!
I have conquered the world.
John 16:33 Holman CSB

Are you a confident, faithful believer, or do you live under a cloud of uncertainty and doubt? As a Christian, you have many reasons to be confident. After all, God is in His heaven; Christ has risen; and you are the recipient of God's grace. Despite these blessings, you may, from time to time, find yourself being tormented by stressful, destructive emotions—and you are certainly not alone.

Even the most faithful Christians are overcome by occasional bouts of fear and doubt. You are no different. But even when you feel very distant from God, remember that God is never distant from you. When you sincerely seek His presence, He will touch your heart, calm your fears, and restore your confidence.

May God help us to express and define ourselves in our one-of-a-kind way.

Luci Swindoll

Confidence in the natural world is self-reliance; in the spiritual world, it is God-reliance.

Oswald Chambers

The more wisdom enters our hearts, the more we will be able to trust our hearts in difficult situations.

John Eldredge

The single most important element in any human relationship is honesty—with oneself, with God, and with others.

Catherine Marshall

Do you lack confidence? If so, pay careful attention to the direction of your thoughts. And while you're at it, pay careful attention to the promises contained in God's Holy Word. Remember: the more you trust God, the more confident you will become.

A PRAYER

Dear Heavenly Father, when I am troubled, You heal me.
When I am afraid, You protect me. When I am discouraged,
You lift me up. In times of adversity, let me trust
Your plan and Your will for my life. And whatever
my circumstances, Lord, let me always give the thanks
and the glory to You. Amen

NOTES TO YOURSELF ABOUT . . .

Your willingness to face tough times with courage,
with confidence, and with God.

Chapter 14

The Wisdom of Moderation

Patience is better than power, and controlling one's temper,
than capturing a city.
Proverbs 16:32 Holman CSB

THOUGHT FOR THE DAY

Overindulgence creates stress; moderation reduces it. Act accordingly.

Moderation and wisdom are traveling companions. If we are wise, we must learn to temper our appetites, our desires, and our impulses. When we do, we are blessed, in part, because God has created a world in which temperance is rewarded and intemperance is inevitably punished.

When we allow our appetites to run wild, they usually do. When we abandon moderation, we forfeit the inner peace that God offers—but does not guarantee—to His children. When we live intemperate lives, we rob ourselves of countless blessings that would have otherwise been ours.

God's instructions are clear: if we seek to live wisely, we must be moderate in our appetites and disciplined in our behavior. To do otherwise is an affront to Him . . . and to ourselves.

Moderation is especially difficult in an excessive society such as ours, but the rewards of moderation are numerous and long-lasting. No one can force you to control your appetites. The decision to live temperately (and wisely) is yours and yours alone. And so are the consequences.

The more we stuff ourselves with material pleasures, the less we seem to appreciate life.

Barbara Johnson

Remember that God's Word instructs you to be moderate and disciplined as you guard your body, your mind, and your heart. So when in doubt, be a little more moderate than necessary.

When I feel like circumstances are spiraling downward in my life, God taught me that whether I'm right side up or upside down, I need to turn those circumstances over to Him. He is the only one who can bring balance into my life.

Carole Lewis

To many, total abstinence is easier than perfect moderation.

St. Augustine

As faithful stewards of what we have, ought we not to give earnest thought to our staggering surplus?

Elisabeth Elliot

The Simple Life

Add to your faith virtue; and to virtue, knowledge;
and to knowledge, temperance; and to temperance, patience;
and to patience, godliness; and to godliness, brotherly kindness;
and to brotherly kindness, charity.
2 Peter 1:5-7 KJV

Want to reduce stress? Here's a simple solution: Simplify your life. Unfortunately, it's easier said than done. After all, you live in a world where simplicity is in short supply.

Think for a moment about the complexity of your everyday life and compare it to the lives of your ancestors. Certainly, you are the beneficiary of many technological innovations, but those innovations have a price: in all likelihood, your world is highly complex. Unless you take firm control of your time and your life, you may be overwhelmed by a stress-inducing tidal wave of complexity that threatens your happiness.

Your Heavenly Father understands the joy of living simply, and so should you. So do yourself a favor: Keep your life as simple as possible. Simplicity is, indeed, genius. By simplifying your life, you are destined to improve it.

Nobody is going to simplify your life for you. You've got to simplify things for yourself.

Marie T. Freeman

The most powerful life is the most simple life. The most powerful life is the life that knows where it's going, that knows where the source of strength is; it is the life that stays free of clutter and happenstance and hurriedness.

Max Lucado

A peaceful heart finds joy in all of life's simple pleasures.

Anonymous

Efficiency is enhanced not by what we accomplish but more often by what we relinquish.

Charles Swindoll

Perhaps you think that the more stuff you acquire, the happier you'll be. If so, think again. Too much stuff means too much stress, so start simplifying now.

A PRAYER

Dear Lord, give me the wisdom to be moderate and self-disciplined. Let me strive to do Your will here on earth, and as I do, let me find contentment and balance. Let me be a disciplined believer, Father, today and every day. Amen

NOTES TO YOURSELF ABOUT . . .
Ways that you can simplify your life.

_____

_____

_____

_____

_____

_____

_____

_____

_____

_____

Chapter 15

Taking Care of Your Body

Do you not know that your body is a sanctuary of the Holy Spirit who is in you, whom you have from God? You are not your own, for you were bought at a price; therefore glorify God in your body.
1 Corinthians 6:19-20 Holman CSB

THOUGHT FOR THE DAY

A healthy lifestyle reduces stress just as surely as an unhealthy lifestyle increases stress. And since your body is a gift from God, why not treat it with the care it deserves?

Poor physical health and stress often go hand-in-hand. That's one reason (but certainly not the only reason) that you should place a high priority on caring for the only body that you'll ever own in this lifetime. And God's willing to help.

If you're concerned with your spiritual, physical, or emotional health, there is a timeless source of comfort and advice that is as near as your bookshelf. That source is the Holy Bible.

God's Word has much to say about every aspect of your life, including your health. If you face personal health challenges that seem almost insoluble, have faith and seek God's wisdom. If you can't seem to get yourself on a sensible diet or on a program of regular physical exercise, consult God's teachings. If your approach to your physical or emotional health has, up to this point, been undisciplined, pray to your Creator for the strength to do what you know is right.

God has given you the Holy Bible for the purpose of knowing His promises, His power, His commandments, His wisdom, His love, and His Son. As you seek to improve the state of your own health, study God's teachings and apply them to your life. When you do, you'll quickly discover that God has the power to change everything, including you.

As you talk to God each morning, ask Him for the strength and the wisdom to treat your body as His creation and His "temple." During the day ahead, you will face countless temptations to do otherwise, but with God's help, you can treat your body as the priceless, one-of-a-kind gift that it most certainly is.

People are funny. When they are young, they will spend their health to get wealth. Later, they will gladly pay all they have trying to get their health back.

John Maxwell

You can't buy good health at the doctor's office—you've got to earn it for yourself.

Marie T. Freeman

Our primary motivation should not be for more energy or to avoid a heart attack but to please God with our bodies.

Carole Lewis

Laughter is jogging for the insides. It increases heart rate and circulation, stimulates the immune system, and improves the muscle tone of the abdomen.

Barbara Johnson

Sensible Exercise Reduces Stress

But I discipline my body and bring it into subjection, lest,
when I have preached to others,
I myself should become disqualified.
1 Corinthians 9:27 NKJV

How much exercise is right for you? That's a decision that you should make in consultation with your physician. But make no mistake: if you sincerely desire to be a thoughtful caretaker of the body that God has given you, exercise is important.

Once you begin a regular exercise program, you'll discover that the benefits to you are not only physical but also psychological. Regular exercise allows you to build your muscles while you're clearing your head and lifting your spirits.

So, if you or your loved ones have been taking your bodies for granted, today is a wonderful day to change. You can start slowly, perhaps with a brisk walk around the block. As your stamina begins to build, so too will your sense of satisfaction. And, you'll be comforted by knowledge that you've done your part to protect and preserve the precious body that God has entrusted to your care.

What's the exercise prescription for today?
Something is better than nothing,
and more is better than something.

—

Dr. Jody Wilkinson

Physical exercise helps relieve stress. And remember that physical, emotional, and spiritual fitness are all part of God's plan for you. But it's up to you to make certain that a healthy lifestyle is a fundamental part of your plan, too.

A PRAYER

Dear Lord, my body is, indeed, a priceless gift from You.
Guide my steps, Father, and help me treat my body
with care today and every day of my life. Amen

NOTES TO YOURSELF ABOUT . . .

Steps you can take to improve your physical,
emotional, or spiritual health.

_____

_____

_____

_____

_____

_____

_____

_____

_____

Chapter 16

Overcommitted?

Rejoice in hope; be patient in affliction; be persistent in prayer.
Romans 12:12 Holman CSB

THOUGHT FOR THE DAY

Trying to do too much—even if your intentions are pure—is a sure way to invite stress into your home. So if you want to avoid stress, avoid over-commitment.

Do you have too many things on your to-do list and too few hours in which to do them? If so, it's time to take a long, hard look at the way you're prioritizing your days and your life.

The world encourages you to rush full-speed ahead, taking on lots of new commitments, doing many things, but doing few things well. God, on the other hand, encourages you to slow down, to quiet yourself, and to spend time with Him. And you can be sure that God's way is best.

How will you organize your life? Will you carve out quiet moments with the Creator? And while you're at it, will you focus your energies and your resources on only the most important tasks on your to-do list? Or will you max out your schedule, leaving much of your most important work undone?

Today, slow yourself down and commit more time to God. When you do, you'll be amazed at how the Father can revolutionize your life when you start spending more time with Him.

Talk to your friends about the drawbacks of being over-committed. Discuss whether it's better to do a few jobs well or many jobs not-so-well. And, talk about the wisdom of saying no to things you simply cannot or should not do.

Life is strenuous.
See that your clock does not run down.

—

Mrs. Charles E. Cowman

Frustration is not the will of God.
There is time to do anything and everything
that God wants us to do.

—

Elisabeth Elliot

Learning to Say No

Therefore since we also have such a large cloud of witnesses surrounding us, let us lay aside every weight and the sin that so easily ensnares us, and run with endurance the race that lies before us.
Hebrews 12:1 Holman CSB

Face facts: If you haven't yet learned to say "No"—to say it politely, firmly, and often—you're inviting untold stress into your life. Why? Because if you can't say "No" (when appropriate) to family members, friends, or coworkers, you'll find yourself overcommitted and under-appreciated.

If you have trouble standing up for yourself, perhaps you're afraid that you'll be rejected. But here's a tip: don't worry too much about rejection, especially when you're rejected for doing the right thing.

Pleasing other people is a good thing . . . up to a point. But you must never allow your "willingness to please" to interfere with your own good judgment or with God's priorities.

God gave you a conscience for a reason: to inform you about the things you need to do as well as the things you don't need to do. It's up to you to follow your conscience wherever it may lead, even if it means making unpopular decisions. Your job, should you choose to accept it, is to be popular with God, not people.

If you are struggling to make some difficult decisions right now that aren't specifically addressed in the Bible, don't make a choice based on what's right for someone else. You are the Lord's and He will make sure you do what's right.

Lisa Whelchel

When we are set free from the bondage of pleasing others, when we are free from currying others' favor and others' approval—then no one will be able to make us miserable or dissatisfied. And then, if we know we have pleased God, contentment will be our consolation.

Kay Arthur

The busier we are, the easier it is to worry, the greater the temptation to worry, the greater the need to be alone with God.

Charles Stanley

Remember that you have a right to say "No" to requests that you consider unreasonable or inconvenient. Don't feel guilty for asserting your right to say "No," and don't feel compelled to fabricate excuses for your decisions.

A PRAYER

Dear Lord, when I'm tired, give me the wisdom to do
the smart thing: give me the wisdom to put my head
on my pillow and rest! Amen

NOTES TO YOURSELF ABOUT . . .

The dangers of over-commitment and the need
to focus on family and faith.

_____

_____

_____

_____

_____

_____

_____

_____

_____

_____

Chapter 17

Worried?

Don't worry about anything, but in everything,
through prayer and petition with thanksgiving,
let your requests be made known to God.
Philippians 4:6 Holman CSB

THOUGHT FOR THE DAY

Needless worry creates needless stress. So when you're troubled,
learn to worry less by trusting God more.

Because we are imperfect human beings struggling with imperfect circumstances, we worry. Even though we, as Christians, have the assurance of salvation—even though we, as Christians, have the promise of God's love and protection—we find ourselves fretting over the inevitable frustrations of everyday life. Jesus understood our concerns when He spoke the reassuring words found in the 6th chapter of Matthew.

Where is the best place to take your worries? Take them to God. Take your troubles to Him; take your fears to Him; take your doubts to Him; take your weaknesses to Him; take your sorrows to Him . . . and leave them all there. Seek protection from the One who offers you eternal salvation; build your spiritual house upon the Rock that cannot be moved.

Perhaps you are concerned about your future, your health, or your finances. Or perhaps you are simply a "worrier" by nature. If so, make Matthew 6 a regular part of your daily Bible reading. This beautiful passage will remind you that God still sits in His heaven and you are His beloved child. Then, perhaps, you will worry a little less and trust God a little more, and that's as it should be because God is trustworthy . . . and you are protected.

Assiduously divide your areas of concern into two categories: those you can control and those you cannot. Resolve
never to waste time or energy worrying about the latter.

Worry is the senseless process of cluttering up tomorrow's
opportunities with leftover problems from today.

Barbara Johnson

We are not called to be burden-bearers, but cross-bearers and
light-bearers. We must cast our burdens on the Lord.

Corrie ten Boom

This life of faith, then, consists in just this—being a child in the
Father's house. Let the ways of childish confidence and freedom
from care, which so please you and win your heart when you
observe your own little ones, teach you what you should be in
your attitude toward God.

Hannah Whitall Smith

Today is mine. Tomorrow is none of my business. If I peer
anxiously into the fog of the future, I will strain my spiritual
eyes so that I will not see clearly what is required of me now.

Elisabeth Elliott

Wisdom in a Donut Shop

My cup runs over. Surely goodness and mercy shall follow me
all the days of my life; and I will dwell
in the house of the Lord Forever.
Psalm 23:5-6 NKJV

On the wall of a little donut shop, the sign said:

As you travel through life, brother,
Whatever be your goal,
Keep your eye upon the donut,
And not upon the hole.

Are you a Christian who keeps your eye upon the donut, or have you acquired the bad habit of looking only at the hole? Hopefully, you spend most of your waking hours looking at the donut (and thanking God for it).

Christianity and pessimism don't mix. So do yourself a favor: choose to be a hope-filled Christian. Think optimistically about your life and your future. Trust your hopes, not your fears. Take time to celebrate God's glorious creation. And then, when you've filled your heart with hope and gladness, share your optimism with your friends. They'll be better for it, and so will you. But not necessarily in that order.

If you can't tell whether your glass is half-empty or half-full, you don't need another glass; what you need is better eyesight . . . and a more thankful heart.

Marie T. Freeman

The Christian lifestyle is not one of legalistic do's and don'ts, but one that is positive, attractive, and joyful.

Vonette Bright

We may run, walk, stumble, drive, or fly, but let us never lose sight of the reason for the journey, or miss a chance to see a rainbow on the way.

Gloria Gaither

It never hurts your eyesight to look on the bright side of things.

Barbara Johnson

Be a realistic optimist. You should strive to think realistically about the future, but you should never confuse realism with pessimism. Your attitude toward the future will help create your future, so you might as well put the self-fulfilling prophecy to work for you by being both a realist and an optimist. And remember that life is far too short to be a pessimist.

A PRAYER

Lord, You sent Your Son to live as a man on this earth,
and You know what it means to be completely human.
You understand my worries and my fears, Lord, and You
forgive me when I am weak. When my faith begins to wane,
help me, Lord, to trust You more. Then, with Your
Holy Word on my lips and with the love of Your Son in
my heart, let me live courageously, faithfully, prayerfully,
and thankfully today and every day. Amen

NOTES TO YOURSELF ABOUT . . .
The futility of worry and the need to trust God.

_____

_____

_____

_____

_____

_____

_____

_____

_____

_____

Chapter 18

Learn the Art of Patience

And we exhort you, brothers: warn those who are lazy,
comfort the discouraged, help the weak, be patient with everyone.
1 Thessalonians 5:14 Holman CSB

THOUGHT FOR THE DAY

If you want to learn how to beat stress, learn how to be more patient.

The dictionary defines the word *patience* as "the ability to be calm, tolerant, and understanding." If that describes you, you can skip the rest of this page. But, if you're like most of us, you'd better keep reading.

For most of us, patience is a hard thing to master. Why? Because we have lots of things we want, and we know precisely when we want them: NOW (if not sooner). But our Father in heaven has other ideas; the Bible teaches that we must learn to wait patiently for the things that God has in store for us, even when waiting is difficult.

We live in an imperfect world inhabited by imperfect people. Sometimes, we inherit troubles from others, and sometimes we create troubles for ourselves. On other occasions, we see other people "moving ahead" in the world, and we want to move ahead with them. So we become impatient with ourselves, with our circumstances, and even with our Creator.

Psalm 37:7 commands us to "rest in the Lord, and wait patiently for Him" (NKJV). But, for most of us, waiting patiently for Him is hard. We are fallible human beings who seek solutions to our problems today, not tomorrow. Still, God instructs us to wait patiently for His plans to unfold, and that's exactly what we should do.

Sometimes, patience is the price we pay for being responsible adults, and that's as it should be. After all, think how patient our Heavenly Father has been with us.

So the next time you find yourself stressfully drumming your fingers as you wait for a quick resolution to the challenges of everyday living, take a deep breath and ask God for patience. Be still before your Heavenly Father and trust His timetable: it's the peaceful way to live.

When you learn to be more patient with others, you'll make your world—and your heart—a more peaceful and less stressful place.

He makes us wait. He keeps us in the dark on purpose. He makes us walk when we want to run, sit still when we want to walk, for he has things to do in our souls that we are not interested in.

Elisabeth Elliot

When we read of the great Biblical leaders, we see that it was not uncommon for God to ask them to wait, not just a day or two, but for years, until God was ready for them to act.

Gloria Gaither

Controlling Your Emotions

Don't abandon wisdom, and she will watch over you;
love her, and she will guard you.
Proverbs 4:6 Holman CSB

Who is in charge of your emotions? Is it you, or have you formed the unfortunate habit of letting other people—or troubling situations—determine the quality of your thoughts and the direction of your day? If you're wise—and if you'd like to build a better life for yourself and your loved ones—you'll learn to control your emotions before your emotions control you.

Human emotions are highly variable, decidedly unpredictable, and often unreliable. Our emotions are like the weather, only far more fickle. So we must learn to live by faith, not by the ups and downs of our own emotional roller coasters.

Sometime during this day, you will probably be gripped by a strong negative feeling. Distrust it. Reign it in. Test it. And turn it over to God. Your emotions will inevitably change; God will not. So trust Him completely as you watch those negative feelings slowly evaporate into thin air—which, of course, they will.

Emotions we have not poured out in the safe hands of God can turn into feelings of hopelessness and depression. God is safe.

Beth Moore

Don't bother much about your feelings. When they are humble, loving, brave, give thanks for them; when they are conceited, selfish, cowardly, ask to have them altered. In neither case are they you, but only a thing that happens to you. What matters is your intentions and your behavior.

C. S. Lewis

Instead of waiting for the feeling, wait upon God. You can do this by growing still and quiet, then expressing in prayer what your mind knows is true about Him, even if your heart doesn't feel it at this moment.

Shirley Dobson

Remember: Your life shouldn't be ruled by your emotions—your life should be ruled by God. So if you think you've lost control over your emotions, don't make big decisions, don't strike out against anybody, and don't speak out in anger. Count to ten (or more) and take "time out" from your situation until you calm down.

A PRAYER

Dear Lord, let me live according to Your plan and according to Your timetable. When I am hurried, Lord, slow me down. When I become impatient with others, give me empathy. Today, Lord, let me be a patient Christian, and let me trust in You and in Your master plan. Amen

NOTES TO YOURSELF ABOUT . . .

Steps you can take to become a more patient person.

_____

_____

_____

_____

_____

_____

_____

_____

_____

_____

Chapter 19

Conquering Everyday Frustrations

A hot-tempered man stirs up conflict,
but a man slow to anger calms strife.
Proverbs 15:18 Holman CSB

THOUGHT FOR THE DAY

Angry thoughts are stress-inducing thoughts. So if you want to defeat stress, you must learn to control your temper before your temper controls you.

A nger is a natural human emotion that is sometimes necessary and appropriate. Even Jesus became angry when confronted with the moneychangers in the temple: "And Jesus entered the temple and drove out all those who were buying and selling in the temple, and overturned the tables of the moneychangers and the seats of those who were selling doves" (Matthew 21:12 NASB). Righteous indignation is an appropriate response to evil, but God does not intend that anger should rule our lives. Far from it. God intends that we turn away from anger whenever possible and forgive our neighbors just as we seek forgiveness for ourselves.

Life is full of stresses and frustrations, some great and some small. On occasion, you, like Jesus, will confront evil, and when you do, you may respond as He did: vigorously and without reservation. But, more often your frustrations will be of the more mundane variety. As long as you live here on earth, you will face countless opportunities to lose your temper over small, relatively insignificant events: a traffic jam, a spilled cup of coffee, an inconsiderate comment, a broken promise. When you are tempted to lose your temper over the minor inconveniences of life, don't. Turn away from anger, hatred, bitterness, and regret. Turn instead to God. When you do, you'll be following His commandments and giving yourself a priceless gift . . . the gift of peace.

Angry words are dangerous to your emotional and spiritual health, not to mention your relationships. So treat anger as an uninvited guest, and usher it away as quickly—and as quietly—as possible.

When something robs you of your peace of mind, ask yourself if it is worth the energy you are expending on it. If not, then put it out of your mind in an act of discipline. Every time the thought of "it" returns, refuse it.

Kay Arthur

Life is too short to spend it being angry, bored, or dull.

Barbara Johnson

Get rid of the poison of built-up anger and the acid of long-term resentment.

Charles Swindoll

Beyond Bitterness

All bitterness, anger and wrath, insult and slander must be removed from you, along with all wickedness. And be kind and compassionate to one another, forgiving one another, just as God also forgave you in Christ.
Ephesians 4:31-32 Holman CSB

Bitterness is a stress-inducing spiritual sickness. It will consume your soul; it is dangerous to your emotional health. It can destroy you if you let it . . . so don't let it!

If you are caught up in intense feelings of anger or resentment, you know all too well the destructive power of these emotions. How can you rid yourself of these feelings? First, you must prayerfully ask God to cleanse your heart. Then, you must learn to catch yourself whenever thoughts of bitterness or hatred begin to attack you. Your challenge is this: You must learn to resist negative thoughts before they hijack your emotions.

Matthew 5:22 teaches us that if we judge our brothers and sisters, we, too, will be subject to judgement. Let us refrain, then, from judging our neighbors. Instead, let us forgive them and love them, while leaving their judgement to a far more capable authority: the One who sits on His throne in heaven.

Grudges are like hand grenades; it is wise to release them before they destroy you.

Barbara Johnson

When you harbor bitterness, happiness will dock elsewhere.

Anonymous

Bitterness is a spiritual cancer, a rapidly growing malignancy that can consume your life. Bitterness cannot be ignored but must be healed at the very core, and only Christ can heal bitterness.

Beth Moore

Sin is any deed or memory that hampers or binds human personality.

Catherine Marshall

Holding a grudge? Drop it! Remember, holding a grudge is like letting somebody live rent-free in your brain . . . so don't do it!

A PRAYER

Dear Lord, when I am angry, I cannot feel the peace that
You intend for my life. When I am bitter, I cannot sense
Your love. Heavenly Father, keep me mindful that
forgiveness is Your commandment and Your will for my life.
Let me turn away from anger and instead claim the spiritual
abundance that You offer through the priceless gift
of Your Son Jesus. Amen

NOTES TO YOURSELF ABOUT . . .

Things that typically make you angry . . . and specific steps
you can take to control your temper.

_____

_____

_____

_____

_____

_____

_____

_____

_____

_____

Chapter 20

Praise Him

Give thanks to the Lord, for He is good;
His faithful love endures forever.
Psalm 106:1 Holman CSB

THOUGHT FOR THE DAY

Want to overcome the stresses of everyday life? Try spending more time thanking God and praising Him for His blessings.

God has blessed us beyond measure, and we owe Him everything, including our constant praise. That's why thanksgiving should become a habit, a regular part of our daily routines. When we slow down and express our gratitude to the One who made us, we enrich our own lives and the lives of those around us.

Dietrich Bonhoeffer observed, "It is only with gratitude that life becomes rich." These words most certainly apply to you.

As a follower of Christ, you have been blessed beyond measure. God sent His only Son to die for you. And, God has given you the priceless gifts of eternal love and eternal life. You, in turn, should approach your Heavenly Father with reverence and gratitude.

Are you a thankful person? Do you appreciate the gifts that God has given you? And, do you demonstrate your gratitude by being a faithful steward of the gifts and talents that you have received from your Creator? You most certainly should be thankful. After all, when you stop to think about it, God has given you more blessings than you can count. So the question of the day is this: will you thank your Heavenly Father . . . or will you spend your time and energy doing other things?

God is always listening—are you willing to say thanks? It's up to you, and the next move is yours.

Thoughtful believers (like you) make it a habit to carve out quiet moments throughout the day to praise God.

Nothing we do is more powerful or more life-changing than praising God.

Stormie Omartian

Our God is the sovereign Creator of the universe! He loves us as His own children and has provided every good thing we have; He is worthy of our praise every moment.

Shirley Dobson

Preoccupy my thoughts with your praise beginning today.

Joni Eareckson Tada

Two wings are necessary to lift our souls toward God: prayer and praise. Prayer asks. Praise accepts the answer.

Mrs. Charles E. Cowman

This Is His Day

This is the day the Lord has made;
let us rejoice and be glad in it.
Psalm 118:24 Holman CSB

God gives us this day; He fills it to the brim with possibilities, and He challenges us to use it for His purposes. The 118th Psalm reminds us that today, like every other day, is a cause for celebration. The day is presented to us fresh and clean at midnight, free of charge, but we must beware: Today is a non-renewable resource—once it's gone, it's gone forever. Our responsibility, of course, is to use this day in the service of God's will and according to His commandments.

Today, treasure the time that God has given you. Give Him the glory and the praise and the thanksgiving that He deserves. And search for the hidden possibilities that God has placed along your path. This day is a priceless gift from God, so use it joyfully and encourage others to do likewise. After all, this is the day the Lord has made . . . .

Every day of our lives we make choices about how we're going to live that day.

Luci Swindoll

Submit each day to God, knowing that He is God over all your tomorrows.

Kay Arthur

Lovely, complicated wrappings Sheath the gift of one-day-more; Breathless, I untie the package— Never lived this day before!

Gloria Gaither

Today is mine. Tomorrow is none of my business. If I peer anxiously into the fog of the future, I will strain my spiritual eyes so that I will not see clearly what is required of me now.

Elisabeth Elliot

If you're too stressed out to celebrate life today, start thanking God for the gifts He has given you. Try counting those gifts one-by-one. When you do, you won't stay stressed for long.

A PRAYER

Heavenly Father, today and every day I will praise You.
I will praise You with my thoughts, my prayers, my words,
and my deeds . . . now and forever. Amen

NOTES TO YOURSELF ABOUT . . .

The blessings that you experience when you praise
God for His gifts.

_____

_____

_____

_____

_____

_____

_____

_____

_____

Chapter 21

The Right Attitude Helps Reduce Stress

Finally brothers, whatever is true, whatever is honorable,
whatever is just, whatever is pure, whatever is lovely,
whatever is commendable—if there is any moral excellence
and if there is any praise—dwell on these things.
Philippians 4:8 Holman CSB

THOUGHT FOR THE DAY

As the old saying goes, your attitude determines your altitude. And your attitude also determines your stress level. So act—and think—accordingly.

How will you direct your thoughts today? Will you obey the words of Philippians 4:8 by dwelling upon those things that are honorable, just, and commendable? Or will you allow your thoughts to be hijacked by the negativity that seems to dominate our troubled world? Are you fearful, angry, stressed, or worried? Are you so preoccupied with the concerns of this day that you fail to thank God for the promise of eternity? Are you confused, bitter, or pessimistic? If so, God wants to have a little talk with you.

God intends that you experience joy and abundance. So, today and every day hereafter, celebrate the life that God has given you by focusing your thoughts upon those things that are worthy of praise. Today, count your blessings instead of your hardships. And thank the Giver of all things good for gifts that are simply too numerous to count.

Today, create a positive attitude by focusing on opportunities, not roadblocks. Of course you may have experienced disappointments in the past, and you will undoubtedly experience some setbacks in the future. But don't invest large amounts of energy focusing on past misfortunes. Instead, look to the future with optimism and hope.

I could go through this day oblivious to the miracles all around me, or I could tune in and "enjoy."

Gloria Gaither

The things we think are the things that feed our souls. If we think on pure and lovely things, we shall grow pure and lovely like them; and the converse is equally true.

Hannah Whitall Smith

The Reference Point for the Christian is the Bible. All values, judgments, and attitudes must be gauged in relationship to this Reference Point.

Ruth Bell Graham

No matter how little we can change about our circumstances, we always have a choice about our attitude toward the situation.

Vonette Bright

Anxious?

Be anxious for nothing, but in everything
by prayer and supplication, with thanksgiving,
let your requests be made known to God.
Philippians 4:6 NKJV

We live in a fast-paced, stress-inducing, anxiety-filled world that oftentimes seems to shift beneath our feet. Sometimes, trusting God is difficult, especially when we become caught up in the incessant demands of an anxious world.

When you feel stressed to the breaking point—and you will—return your thoughts to God's love and God's promises. And as you confront the challenges of everyday living, turn all of your concerns over to your Heavenly Father.

The same God who created the universe will comfort and guide you if you ask Him . . . so ask Him. Then watch in amazement as your anxieties melt into the warmth of His loving hands.

So often we pray and then fret anxiously, waiting for God to hurry up and do something. All the while God is waiting for us to calm down, so He can do something through us.

Corrie ten Boom

Worship and worry cannot live in the same heart; they are mutually exclusive.

Ruth Bell Graham

We must lay our questions, frustrations, anxieties, and impotence at the feet of God and wait for His answer. And then receiving it, we must live by faith.

Kay Arthur

Never yield to gloomy anticipation. Place your hope and confidence in God. He has no record of failure.

Mrs. Charles E. Cowman

Remembering God's faithfulness in the past can give you peace for today and hope for tomorrow.

A PRAYER

Lord, sometimes this world is a difficult place, and,
as a frail human being, I am fearful. When I am worried,
restore my faith. When I am anxious, turn my thoughts to
You. When I endure stressful times, touch my heart with
Your enduring love. And, keep me mindful, Lord,
that nothing, absolutely nothing, will happen this day
that You and I cannot handle together. Amen

NOTES TO YOURSELF ABOUT . . .

The rewards of optimism and the futility of negativity.

_____

_____

_____

_____

_____

_____

_____

_____

_____

Chapter 22

He Is Sufficient

The Lord is my rock, my fortress, and my deliverer.
Psalm 18:2 Holman CSB

THOUGHT FOR THE DAY

Are you worried or stressed? Remember that God is sufficient
to meet your every need.

I t is easy to become overwhelmed by the demands of everyday life, but if you're a faithful follower of the One from Galilee, you need never be overwhelmed. Why? Because God's love is sufficient to meet your needs. Whatever stresses you may face, whatever heartbreaks you must endure, God is with you, and He stands ready to comfort you and to heal you.

The Psalmist writes, "Weeping may endure for a night, but joy comes in the morning" (Psalm 30:5 NKJV). But when we are suffering, the morning may seem very far away. It is not. God promises that He is "near to those who have a broken heart" (Psalm 34:18 NKJV).

If you are experiencing the intense pain of a recent loss, or if you are still mourning a loss from long ago, perhaps you are now ready to begin the next stage of your journey with God. If so, be mindful of this fact: the loving heart of God is sufficient to meet any challenge, including yours.

God is, must be, our answer to every question and every cry of need.

Hannah Whitall Smith

Focus on possibilities, not stumbling blocks. Of course you will encounter occasional disappointments, and, from time to time, you will encounter failure. But, don't invest large quantities of your life focusing on past misfortunes. Instead, look to the future with optimism and hope ... and encourage your friends and family members to do the same.

God is always sufficient in perfect proportion to our need.

Beth Moore

God uses our most stumbling, faltering faith-steps as the open door to His doing for us "more than we ask or think."

Catherine Marshall

We have ample evidence that the Lord is able to guide. The promises cover every imaginable situation. All we need to do is to take the hand he stretches out.

Elisabeth Elliot

Finding Peace

These things I have spoken to you, that in Me you may have peace.
In the world you will have tribulation;
but be of good cheer, I have overcome the world.
John 16:33 NKJV

Oftentimes, our outer struggles are simply manifestations of the inner conflict that we feel when we stray from God's path. Jesus offers us peace, not as the world gives, but as He alone gives. Our challenge is to accept Christ's peace into our hearts and then, as best we can, to share His peace with our neighbors. When we accept Jesus as our personal Savior, we are transformed by His grace. We are then free to accept the spiritual abundance and peace that can be ours through the power of the risen Christ.

Have you found the genuine peace that can be yours through Jesus Christ? Or are you still rushing after the illusion of "peace and happiness" that the world promises but cannot deliver? Today, as a gift to yourself, to your family, and to your friends, claim the inner peace that is your spiritual birthright: the peace of Jesus Christ. It is offered freely; it has been paid for in full; it is yours for the asking. So ask. And then share.

Prayer guards hearts and minds and causes God to bring peace out of chaos.

Beth Moore

When we do what is right, we have contentment, peace, and happiness.

Beverly LaHaye

To know God as He really is—in His essential nature and character—is to arrive at a citadel of peace that circumstances may storm, but can never capture.

Catherine Marshall

The fruit of our placing all things in God's hands is the presence of His abiding peace in our hearts.

Hannah Whitall Smith

Do you want to discover God's peace? Then do your best to live in the center of God's will.

A PRAYER

Lord, You have promised never to leave me or forsake me.
You are always with me, protecting me and encouraging me.
Whatever this day may bring, I thank You for Your love
and for Your strength. Let me lean upon You, Father,
this day and forever. Amen

NOTES TO YOURSELF ABOUT . . .

God's power to meet your needs.

_____

_____

_____

_____

_____

_____

_____

_____

_____

Chapter 23

Cheerfulness 101

A cheerful heart has a continual feast.
Proverbs 15:15 Holman CSB

THOUGHT FOR THE DAY

Warning: Stress and cheerfulness don't usually coexist in the same human heart.

Cheerfulness is a wonderful antidote to stress. And, as believers who have been saved by a risen Christ, why shouldn't we be cheerful? The answer, of course, is that we have every reason to honor our Savior with joy in our hearts, smiles on our faces, and words of celebration on our lips.

Few things in life are more sad, or, for that matter, more absurd, than the sight of grumpy Christians trudging unhappily through life. Christ promises us lives of abundance and joy if we accept His love and His grace. Yet sometimes, even the most righteous among us are beset by fits of ill temper and frustration. During these moments, we may not feel like turning our thoughts and prayers to Christ, but that's precisely what we should do.

Mrs. Charles E. Cowman, the author of the classic devotional text *Streams in the Desert*, wrote, "Two wings are necessary to lift our souls toward God: prayer and praise. Prayer asks. Praise accepts the answer." That's why we should find the time to lift our concerns to God in prayer, and to praise Him for all that He has done. When we do so, we simply can't stay stressed for long.

God is good, and heaven is forever. And if those two facts don't cheer you up, nothing will.

Marie T. Freeman

Do you need a little cheering up? If so, find somebody else who needs cheering up, too. Then, do your best to brighten that person's day. When you do, you'll discover that cheering up other people is a wonderful way to cheer yourself up, too!

We may run, walk, stumble, drive, or fly, but let us never lose sight of the reason for the journey, or miss a chance to see a rainbow on the way.

Gloria Gaither

When we bring sunshine into the lives of others, we're warmed by it ourselves. When we spill a little happiness, it splashes on us.

Barbara Johnson

The people whom I have seen succeed best in life have always been cheerful and hopeful people who went about their business with a smile on their faces.

Charles Kingsley

A Dose of Laughter

A joyful heart is good medicine,
but a broken spirit dries up the bones.
Proverbs 17:22 Holman CSB

Laughter is medicine for the soul (not to mention a fabulous stress-reducer), but sometimes, amid the challenges of the day, we forget to take our medicine. Instead of viewing our world with a mixture of optimism and humor, we allow worries and distractions to rob us of the joy that God intends for our lives.

Today, as you go about your daily activities, approach life with a smile and a chuckle. After all, God created laughter for a reason . . . and Father indeed knows best. So laugh!

As you're rushing through life, take time to stop a moment, look into people's eyes, say something kind, and try to make them laugh!

Barbara Johnson

I think everybody ought to be a laughing Christian. I'm convinced that there's just one place where there's not any laughter, and that's hell.

Jerry Clower

It is often just as sacred to laugh as it is to pray.

Charles Swindoll

I want to encourage you in these days with your family to lighten up and enjoy. Laugh a little bit; it might just set you free.

Dennis Swanberg

If you can't see the joy and humor in everyday life, you're not paying attention to the right things. Remember the donut-maker's creed: "As you travel through life brother, whatever be your goal, keep your eye upon the donut, and not upon the hole."

A PRAYER

Dear Lord, You have given me so many reasons to be happy,
and I want to be a cheerful Christian. Today and every day,
I will do my best to share my happiness with
my family and my friends. Amen

NOTES TO YOURSELF ABOUT . . .

The rewards of a cheerful disposition.

Chapter 24

In His Hands

Do not boast about tomorrow,
for you do not know what a day may bring forth.
Proverbs 27:1 NKJV

THOUGHT FOR THE DAY

With God as your partner, you can overcome any obstacle.
When you place your future in God's hands, you have absolutely
nothing to fear.

Because we are saved by a risen Christ, we can have hope for the future, no matter how troublesome our present circumstances may seem. After all, God has promised that we are His throughout eternity. And, He has told us that we must place our hopes in Him.

Of course, we will face disappointments and failures while we are here on earth, but these are only temporary defeats. This world can be a place of stresses, trials, and tribulations, but when we place our trust in the Giver of all things good, we are secure. God has promised us peace, joy, and eternal life. And God keeps His promises today, tomorrow, and forever.

Are you willing to place your future in the hands of a loving and all-knowing God? Do you trust in the ultimate goodness of His plan for your life? Will you face today's challenges with optimism and hope? You should. After all, God created you for a very important purpose: His purpose. And you still have important work to do: His work.

Today, as you live in the present and look to the future, remember that God has a plan for you. Act—and believe—accordingly.

Every saint has a past—every sinner has a future!

Anonymous

Today, try to focus more on future opportunities than on past disappointments.

You can look forward with hope, because one day there will be no more separation, no more scars, and no more suffering in My Father's House. It's the home of your dreams!

Anne Graham Lotz

The future lies all before us. Shall it only be a slight advance upon what we usually do? Ought it not to be a bound, a leap forward to altitudes of endeavor and success undreamed of before?

Annie Armstrong

Allow your dreams a place in your prayers and plans. God-given dreams can help you move into the future He is preparing for you.

Barbara Johnson

Discovering God's Plans

*For it is God who is working among you both the willing
and the working for His good purpose.*
Philippians 2:13 Holman CSB

Do you want to experience a life filled with abundance and peace? If so, here's a word of warning: you'll need to resist the temptation to do things "your way" and commit, instead, to do things God's way.

God has plans for your life. Big plans. But He won't force you to follow His will; to the contrary, He has given you free will, the ability to make decisions on your own. With the freedom to choose comes the responsibility of living with the consequences of the choices you make.

The most important decision of your life is, of course, your commitment to accept Jesus Christ as your personal Lord and Savior. And once your eternal destiny is secured, you will undoubtedly ask yourself the question "What now, Lord?" If you earnestly seek God's will for your life, you will find it . . . in time.

Sometimes, God's plans are crystal clear, but other times, He leads you through the wilderness before He delivers you to the Promised Land. So be patient, keep searching, and keep praying. If you do, then in time, God will answer your prayers and make His plans known.

God is right here, and He intends to use you in wonderful, unexpected ways. You'll discover those plans by doing things His way . . . and you'll be eternally grateful that you did.

Nothing happens by happenstance. I am not in the hands of fate, nor am I the victim of man's whims or the devil's ploys. There is One who sits above man, above Satan, and above all heavenly hosts as the ultimate authority of all the universe. That One is my God and my Father!

Kay Arthur

When the dream of our heart is one that God has planted there, a strange happiness flows into us. At that moment, all of the spiritual resources of the universe are released to help us. Our praying is then at one with the will of God and becomes a channel for the Creator's purposes for us and our world.

Catherine Marshall

God has a wonderful plan for your life. And the time to start looking for that plan—and living it—is now. And remember: Discovering God's plan begins with prayer.

A PRAYER

Dear Lord, as I look to the future, I will place my trust in
You. If I become discouraged, I will turn to You. If I am
weak, I will seek strength in You. You are my Father,
and I will place my hope, my trust,
and my faith in You. Amen

NOTES TO YOURSELF ABOUT . . .

Your need to accept the past and look to the future.

_____

_____

_____

_____

_____

_____

_____

_____

_____

_____

Chapter 25

Seeking God's Guidance

Those who are blessed by Him will inherit the land.

Psalm 37:22 Holman CSB

THOUGHT FOR THE DAY

If you'd like a prescription for relieving stress—or for solving any other problem—ask God. When it comes to life's toughest dilemmas, God has all the right solutions.

When we genuinely seek to know the heart of God—when we prayerfully seek His wisdom and His will—our Heavenly Father carefully guides us over the peaks and valleys of life. And as Christians, we can be comforted: Whether we find ourselves at the pinnacle of the mountain or the darkest depths of the valley, the loving heart of God is always there with us.

As Christians whose salvation has been purchased by the blood of Christ, we have every reason to live joyously and courageously. After all, Christ has already fought and won our battle for us—He did so on the cross at Calvary. But despite Christ's sacrifice, and despite God's promises, we may become confused or disoriented by the endless complications and countless distractions of life.

C. S. Lewis observed, "I don't doubt that the Holy Spirit guides your decisions from within when you make them with the intention of pleasing God. The error would be to think that He speaks only within, whereas in reality He speaks also through Scripture, the Church, Christian friends, and books." These words remind us that God has many ways to make Himself known. Our challenge is to make ourselves open to His instruction.

Do you place a high value on God's guidance, and do you talk to Him regularly about matters great and small? Or do you talk with God on a haphazard basis? If you're wise, you'll form the habit of speaking to God early and often. But you won't stop there—you'll also study God's Word, you'll obey God's commandments, and you'll associate with people who do likewise.

So, if you're unsure of your next step, lean upon God's promises and lift your prayers to Him. Remember that God is always near—always trying to get His message through. Open yourself to Him every day, and trust Him to guide your path. When you do, you'll be protected today, tomorrow, and forever.

If you sincerely want to reduce the stress in your life, pray for God's guidance and ask for God's help. When you ask, He will answer.

Are you serious about wanting God's guidance to become a personal reality in your life? The first step is to tell God that you know you can't manage your own life; that you need his help.

Catherine Marshall

I believe that the Creator of this universe takes delight in turning the terrors and tragedies that come with living in this old, fallen domain of the devil and transforming them into something that strengthens our hope, tests our faith, and shows forth His glory.

Al Green

Today Is a New Beginning

You are being renewed in the spirit of your minds;
you put on the new man, the one created according
to God's likeness in righteousness and purity of the truth.
Ephesians 4:23-24 Holman CSB

Each new day offers countless opportunities to serve God, to seek His will, and to obey His teachings. But each day also offers countless opportunities to stray from God's commandments and to wander far from His path.

Sometimes, we wander aimlessly in a wilderness of our own making, but God has better plans of us. And, whenever we ask Him to renew our strength and guide our steps, He does so.

Consider this day a new beginning. Consider it a fresh start, a renewed opportunity to serve your Creator with willing hands and a loving heart. Ask God to renew your sense of purpose as He guides your steps. Today is a glorious opportunity to serve God. Seize that opportunity while you can; tomorrow may indeed be too late.

He is the God of wholeness and restoration.

Stormie Omartian

Repentance removes old sins and wrong attitudes, and it opens the way for the Holy Spirit to restore our spiritual health.

Shirley Dobson

God gives us permission to forget our past and the understanding to live our present. He said He will remember our sins no more. (Psalm 103:11-12)

Serita Ann Jakes

God specializes in things fresh and firsthand. His plans for you this year may outshine those of the past. He's prepared to fill your days with reasons to give Him praise.

Joni Eareckson Tada

God wants to give you peace, and He wants to renew your spirit. It's up to you to slow down and give Him a chance to do so.

A PRAYER

Dear Lord, You always stand ready to guide me.
Let me accept Your guidance, today and every day
of my life. Lead me, Father, so that my life can be
a tribute to Your grace, to Your mercy, to Your love,
and to Your Son. Amen

NOTES TO YOURSELF ABOUT . . .

How God has guided you in the past . . . and how you
intend to let Him guide you in the future.

_____

_____

_____

_____

_____

_____

_____

_____

_____

Chapter 26

Worship Him

I rejoiced with those who said to me,
"Let us go to the house of the Lord."
Psalm 122:1 Holman CSB

THOUGHT FOR THE DAY

Want to keep things in perspective while you're reducing the stresses of everyday life? Try worshipping God seven days a week, not just on Sunday.

If you really want to know God, you must be willing to worship Him seven days a week, not just on Sunday. When you do, you'll discover that heartfelt worship is a wonderful antidote to the stressors of everyday life.

Every life, including yours, is based upon some form of worship. The question is not whether you will worship, but what you worship.

If you choose to worship God, you will receive a bountiful harvest of joy, peace, and abundance. But if you distance yourself from God by foolishly worshiping earthly possessions and personal gratification, you're making a huge mistake. So do this: Worship God today and every day. Worship Him with sincerity and thanksgiving. Write His name on your heart and rest assured that He, too, has written your name on His.

When you worship God with a sincere heart, He will guide your steps, calm your fears, and bless your life.

In the sanctuary, we discover beauty: the beauty of His presence.

Kay Arthur

God asks that we worship Him with our concentrated minds as well as with our wills and emotions. A divided and scattered mind is not effective.

Catherine Marshall

Worship and worry cannot live in the same heart; they are mutually exclusive.

Ruth Bell Graham

To worship Him in truth means to worship Him honestly, without hypocrisy, standing open and transparent before Him.

Anne Graham Lotz

Trusting God

It is better to take refuge in the Lord than to trust in man.
Psalm 118:8 Holman CSB

Sometimes the future seems bright, and sometimes it does not. Yet even when we cannot see the possibilities of tomorrow, God can. As believers, our challenge is to trust an uncertain future to an all-powerful God.

When we trust God, we should trust Him without reservation. We should steel ourselves against the inevitable stresses of the day, secure in the knowledge that our Heavenly Father has a plan for the future that only He can see.

Can you place your future into the hands of a loving and all-knowing God? Can you live amid the uncertainties of today, knowing that God has dominion over all your tomorrows? If you can, you are wise and you are blessed. When you trust God with everything you are and everything you have, He will bless you now and forever.

Sometimes the very essence of faith is trusting God in the midst of things He knows good and well we cannot comprehend.

Beth Moore

Are you serious about wanting God's guidance to become the person he wants you to be? The first step is to tell God that you know you can't manage your own life; that you need his help.

Catherine Marshall

Never be afraid to trust an unknown future to a known God.

Corrie ten Boom

Brother, is your faith looking upward today? Trust in the promise of the Savior. Sister, is the light shining bright on your way? Trust in the promise of thy Lord.

Fanny Crosby

One of the most important lessons that you can ever learn is to trust God for everything—not some things, not most things . . . everything! The more you trust God, the more easily you can overcome the inevitable stresses of everyday life.

A PRAYER

Dear Lord, this world is a place of distractions and temptations. But when I worship You, Father, You set my path—and my heart—straight. Let this day and every day be a time of worship. Help me find quiet moments to praise You for Your blessings, for Your love, and for Your Son. Amen

NOTES TO YOURSELF ABOUT . . .

The role that worship does play in your life . . .
and the role that it should play.

_____

_____

_____

_____

_____

_____

_____

_____

_____

_____

Chapter 27

Beyond Failure

For a righteous man may fall seven times and rise again.
Proverbs 24:16 NKJV

THOUGHT FOR THE DAY

If you're experiencing setbacks or hardships, don't hit the panic button, and don't overreact. And remember this: Real success has little to do with worldly goods or societal status. Genuine success depends upon your relationship with God and His only begotten Son. Period.

The occasional disappointments and failures of life are inevitable. Such setbacks are simply the price that we must occasionally pay for our willingness to take risks as we follow our dreams. But even when we encounter bitter disappointments, we must never lose faith.

The reassuring words of Hebrews 10:36 remind us that when we persevere, we will eventually receive that which God has promised. What's required is perseverance, not perfection.

When we encounter the inevitable difficulties and stresses of life here on earth, God stands ready to protect us. Our responsibility, of course, is to ask Him for protection. When we call upon Him in heartfelt prayer, He will answer—in His own time and according to His own plan—and He will heal us. And, while we are waiting for God's plans to unfold and for His healing touch to restore us, we can be comforted in the knowledge that our Creator can overcome any obstacle, even if we cannot.

If you're willing to repair your life, God is willing to help. If you're not willing to repair your life, God is willing to wait.

Marie T. Freeman

Failure isn't permanent . . . unless you fail to get back up. So pick yourself up, dust yourself off, and trust God. Warren Wiersbe had this advice: "No matter how badly we have failed, we can always get up and begin again. Our God is the God of new beginnings." And don't forget: the best time to begin again is now.

God is able to take mistakes, when they are committed to Him, and make of them something for our good and for His glory.

Ruth Bell Graham

As you place yourself under the sovereign lordship of Jesus Christ, each mistake or failure can lead you right back to the throne.

Barbara Johnson

Failure is one of life's most powerful teachers. How we handle our failures determines whether we're going to simply "get by" in life or "press on."

Beth Moore

When Our Plans Don't Work Out

Haven't I commanded you: be strong and courageous?
Do not be afraid or discouraged,
for the Lord your God is with you wherever you go.
Joshua 1:9 Holman CSB

Some of our most important dreams are the ones we abandon. Some of our most important goals are the ones we don't attain. Sometimes, our most important journeys are the ones that we take to the winding conclusion of what seem to be dead-end streets. Thankfully, with God there are no dead-ends; there are only opportunities to learn, to yield, to trust, to serve, and to grow.

The next time you experience one of life's inevitable disappointments, don't despair and don't be afraid to try "Plan B." Consider every setback an opportunity to choose a different, more appropriate path. Have faith that God may indeed be leading you in an entirely different direction, a direction of His choosing. And as you take your next step, remember that what looks like a dead-end to you may, in fact, be the fast lane according to God.

The difference between winning and losing is how we choose to react to disappointment.

Barbara Johnson

Often God has to shut a door in our face so that he can subsequently open the door through which he wants us to go.

Catherine Marshall

Why should I ever resist any delay or disappointment, any affliction or oppression or humiliation, when I know God will use it in my life to make me like Jesus and to prepare me for heaven?

Kay Arthur

Don't spend too much time asking, "Why me, Lord?" Instead, ask, "What now, Lord?" and then get to work. When you do, you'll feel much better.

A PRAYER

Dear Lord, when I encounter failures and disappointments,
keep me mindful that You are in control. Let me persevere—
even if my soul is troubled—and let me follow Your Son,
Jesus Christ, this day and forever. Amen

NOTES TO YOURSELF ABOUT . . .
Your need to pick yourself up, dust yourself off,
and trust God.

_____

_____

_____

_____

_____

_____

_____

_____

_____

Chapter 28

Living on Purpose

You will show me the path of life; in Your presence is fullness of joy;
at Your right hand are pleasures forevermore.
Psalm 16:11 NKJV

THOUGHT FOR THE DAY

If your life has been turned upside down, you may find yourself searching for something new: a different direction, a new purpose, or a fresh start. As you make your plans, be sure to consult God because even now He is leading you toward a goal that only He can see. Your task is to pray, to listen, and to follow His lead.

Life is best lived on purpose, not by accident: the sooner we discover what God intends for us to do with our lives, the better. But God's purposes aren't always clear to us. Sometimes we wander aimlessly in a wilderness of our own making. And sometimes, we struggle mightily against God in a vain effort to find success and happiness through our own means, not His.

Whenever we struggle against God's plans, we invite stresses into our lives. When we resist God's calling, our efforts bear little fruit. Our best strategy, therefore, is to seek God's wisdom and to follow Him wherever He chooses to lead. When we do so, we are blessed.

When we align ourselves with God's purposes, we avail ourselves of His power and His peace. But how can we know precisely what God's intentions are? The answer, of course, is that even the most well-intentioned believers face periods of uncertainty and doubt about the direction of their lives. So, too, will you.

When you arrive at one of life's inevitable crossroads, that is precisely the moment when you should turn your thoughts and prayers toward God. When you do, He will make Himself known to you in a time and manner of His choosing.

Are you earnestly seeking to discern God's purpose for your life? If so, these pages are intended as a reminder of several important facts: 1. God has a plan for your life; 2. If you seek that plan sincerely and prayerfully, you will find it; 3. When you discover God's purpose for your life, you will experience abundance, peace, joy, and power—God's power. And that's the only kind of power that really matters.

> God has a plan for your life, a definite purpose that you can fulfill . . . or not. Your challenge is to pray for God's guidance and to follow wherever He leads.

Yesterday is just experience but tomorrow is glistening with purpose—and today is the channel leading from one to the other.

Barbara Johnson

Only God's chosen task for you will ultimately satisfy. Do not wait until it is too late to realize the privilege of serving Him in His chosen position for you.

Beth Moore

In the very place where God has put us, whatever its limitations, whatever kind of work it may be, we may indeed serve the Lord Christ.

Elisabeth Elliot

Using Your Talents

Do not neglect the gift that is in you.
1 Timothy 4:14 NKJV

God gives each of us a unique assortment of talents and opportunities. And our Heavenly Father instructs us to be faithful stewards of the gifts that He bestows upon us. But we live in a world that encourages us to do otherwise.

Ours is a society that is filled to the brim with countless opportunities to squander our time, our resources, and our talents. So we must be watchful for distractions and temptations that might lead us astray.

God has blessed you with unique opportunities to serve Him, and He has given you every tool that you need to do so. Today, accept this challenge: value the talent that God has given you, nourish it, make it grow, and share it with the world. After all, the best way to say "Thank You" for God's gifts is to use them.

Not everyone possesses boundless energy or a conspicuous talent. We are not equally blessed with great intellect or physical beauty or emotional strength. But we have all been given the same ability to be faithful.

Gigi Graham Tchividjian

Employ whatever God has entrusted you with, in doing good, all possible good, in every possible kind and degree.

John Wesley

God has given you special talents—now it's your turn to give them back to God.

Marie T. Freeman

You are the only person on earth who can use your ability.

Zig Ziglar

It's both stressful and futile to squander God's blessings. You are the sole owner of your own set of talents and opportunities. God has given you your own particular gifts—the rest is up to you.

A PRAYER

Dear Lord, I know that You have a purpose for my life,
and I will seek that purpose today and every day that I live.
Let my actions be pleasing to You, and let me share
Your Good News with a world that so desperately needs
Your healing hand and the salvation of Your Son. Amen

NOTES TO YOURSELF ABOUT . . .

The way that you're currently using the talents
and opportunities that God has given you.

_____

_____

_____

_____

_____

_____

_____

_____

_____

_____

Chapter 29

God's Guidebook

Your word is a lamp to my feet and a light to my path.
Psalm 119:105 NKJV

THOUGHT FOR THE DAY

Regular Bible study is a powerful tool for maintaining perspective and moderating stress. So turn to the Word every day for guidance, for inspiration, and for Truth with a capital T.

Another great stress reliever is Bible study. God's Word is unlike any other book. The words of Matthew 4:4 remind us that, "Man shall not live by bread alone but by every word that proceedeth out of the mouth of God" (KJV). As believers, we are instructed to study the Bible and meditate upon its meaning for our lives, yet far too many Bibles are laid aside by well-intentioned believers who would like to study the Bible if they could "just find the time."

Warren Wiersbe observed, "When the child of God looks into the Word of God, he sees the Son of God. And, he is transformed by the Spirit of God to share in the glory of God." God's Holy Word is, indeed, a life-changing, stress-reducing, one-of-a-kind treasure. And it's up to you—and only you—to use it that way.

Read your Bible every morning. When you start each day by studying God's Word, you'll change the quality and direction of your life.

Study the Bible and observe how the persons behaved and how God dealt with them. There is explicit teaching on every condition of life.

Corrie ten Boom

Only through routine, regular exposure to God's Word can you and I draw out the nutrition needed to grow a heart of faith.

Elizabeth George

Knowing God involves an intimate, personal relationship that is developed over time through prayer and getting answers to prayer, through Bible study and applying its teaching to our lives, through obedience and experiencing the power of God, through moment-by-moment submission to Him that results in a moment-by-moment filling of the Holy Spirit.

Anne Graham Lotz

The Bible is a remarkable commentary on perspective. Through its divine message, we are brought face to face with issues and tests in daily living and how, by the power of the Holy Spirit, we are enabled to respond positively to them.

Luci Swindoll

His Promises

God—His way is perfect; the word of the Lord is pure.
He is a shield to all who take refuge in Him.
Psalm 18:30 Holman CSB

What do you expect from the day ahead? Are you willing to trust God completely, or are you living beneath a cloud of doubt and fear? God's Word makes it clear: you should trust Him and His promises, and when you do, you can live courageously.

For thoughtful Christians, every day begins and ends with God's Son and God's promises. When we accept Christ into our hearts, God promises us the opportunity for earthly peace and spiritual abundance. But more importantly, God promises us the priceless gift of eternal life.

Sometimes, especially when we find ourselves caught in the inevitable entanglements of life, we fail to trust God completely.

Are you tired? Discouraged? Fearful? Be comforted and trust the promises that God has made to you. Are you worried or stressed? Be confident in God's power. Do you see a difficult future ahead? Be courageous and call upon God. He will protect you and then use you according to His purposes. Are you confused? Listen to the quiet voice of your Heavenly Father. He is not a God of confusion. Talk with Him; listen to Him; trust Him, and trust His promises. He is steadfast, and He is your Protector . . . forever.

Gather the riches of God's promises which can strengthen you in the time when there will be no freedom.

Corrie ten Boom

We have ample evidence that the Lord is able to guide. The promises cover every imaginable situation. All we need to do is to take the hand he stretches out.

Elisabeth Elliot

No one who has ever set out to test God's promises fairly, thoroughly, and humbly has ever had to report that God's promises don't work. On the contrary, given a fair opportunity, God always surprises and overwhelms those who truly seek His bounty and His power.

Peter Marshall

Do you really trust God's promises, or are you hedging your bets? Today, think about the role that God's Word plays in your life, and think about ways that you can worry less and trust God more.

A PRAYER

As we journey through this life, Lord, help us always to
consult the true road map: Your Holy Word. We know
that when we turn our hearts and our thoughts to You,
Father, You will lead us along the path that is right for us.
Today, Dear Lord, let us know Your will and study Your
Word so that we might understand Your plan
for our lives. Amen

NOTES TO YOURSELF ABOUT . . .

What God's Word means to you.

_____

_____

_____

_____

_____

_____

_____

_____

_____

_____

Chapter 30

Who Rules Your Heart?

*For God loved the world in this way: He gave His only Son,
so that everyone who believes in Him will not perish
but have eternal life.*
John 3:16 Holman CSB

THOUGHT FOR THE DAY

The ultimate choice is your choice to welcome God's Son into your heart and by doing so, accept the gift of eternal life. If you haven't already done so, make that choice today.

Your decision to allow Christ to reign over your heart is the pivotal decision of your life. It is a decision that you cannot ignore. It is a decision that is yours and yours alone.

God's love for you is deeper and more profound than you can imagine. God's love for you is so great that He sent His only Son to this earth to die for your sins and to offer you the priceless gift of eternal life. Now, you must decide whether or not to accept God's gift. Will you ignore it or embrace it? Will you return it or neglect it? Will you accept Christ's love and build a lifelong relationship with Him, or will you turn away from Him and take a different path?

Accept God's gift now: allow His Son to preside over your heart, your thoughts, and your life, starting this very instant.

Your relationship with Jesus should change everything, including the way you view the inevitable stresses of everyday life.

The amount of power you experience to live a victorious, triumphant Christian life is directly proportional to the freedom you give the Spirit to be Lord of your life!

Anne Graham Lotz

Turn your life over to Christ today, and your life will never be the same.

Billy Graham

The most profound essence of my nature is that I am capable of receiving God.

St. Augustine

Choose Jesus Christ! Deny yourself, take up the Cross, and follow Him—for the world must be shown. The world must see, in us, a discernible, visible, startling difference.

Elisabeth Elliot

It's your heart that Jesus longs for: your will to be made His own with self on the cross forever, and Jesus alone on the throne.

Ruth Bell Graham

Let Jesus Guide the Way

I have come as a light into the world,
so that everyone who believes in Me would not
remain in darkness.
John 12:46 Holman CSB

Would you like a proven formula for overcoming the concerns and stress of everyday life? Here's a formula that is proven and true: Make Jesus the cornerstone of your life. Start your day with Him, walk with Him, speak with Him often, and trust His promises.

Thomas Brooks spoke for believers of every generation when he observed, "Christ is the sun, and all the watches of our lives should be set by the dial of his motion." Christ, indeed, is the ultimate Savior of mankind and the personal Savior of those who believe in Him. As His servants, we should place Him at the very center of our lives. And every day that God gives us breath, we should share Christ's love and His message with a world that needs both.

How awesome that the "Word" that was in the beginning, by which and through which God created everything, was—and is—a living Person with a mind, will, emotions, and intellect.

Anne Graham Lotz

When we are in a situation where Jesus is all we have, we soon discover he is all we really need.

Gigi Graham Tchividjian

In your greatest weakness, turn to your greatest strength, Jesus, and hear Him say, "My grace is sufficient for you, for My strength is made perfect in weakness" (2 Corinthians 12:9, NKJV).

Lisa Whelchel

Tell me the story of Jesus. Write on my heart every word. Tell me the story most precious, sweetest that ever was heard.

Fanny Crosby

If you're trying to mold your relationship with Jesus into something that fits comfortably into your own schedule and your own personal theology, you may be headed for trouble. A far better strategy is this: conform yourself to Jesus, not vice versa.

A PRAYER

Father, You gave Your Son that I might have life eternal.
Thank You for this priceless gift and for the joy I feel in
my heart when I give You my thoughts, my prayers,
my praise, and my life. Amen

NOTES TO YOURSELF ABOUT . . .

Steps that you can take today to follow in the footsteps
of God's Son.

_____

_____

_____

_____

_____

_____

_____

_____

_____

_____

More Important
Ideas for
Beating Stress

Understand Depression

Why am I so depressed? Why this turmoil within me? Put your hope in God, for I will still praise Him, my Savior and my God.
Psalm 42:11 Holman CSB

It has been said, and with good reason, that depression is the common cold of mental illness. Why? Because depression is such a common malady. But make no mistake: depression is a serious condition that, if untreated, can take a terrible toll on individuals and families alike.

The sadness that accompanies any significant loss is an inescapable fact of life. Throughout our lives, all of us must endure the kinds of deep personal losses that leave us struggling to find hope. But in time, we move beyond our grief as the sadness runs its course and gradually abates.

Depression, on the other hand, is a physical and emotional condition that is, in almost all cases, treatable with medication and counseling. Depression is not a disease to be taken lightly. Left untreated, it presents real dangers to patients' physical health and to their emotional well-being.

If you find yourself feeling "blue," perhaps it's a logical reaction to the ups and downs of daily life. But if your feelings of sadness have lasted longer than you think they should—or if someone close to you fears that your sadness may have evolved into clinical depression—it's time to seek professional help.

Here are a few simple guidelines to consider as you make decisions about possible medical treatment:

1. If you have persistent urges toward self-destructive behavior, or if you feel as though you have lost the will to live, consult a professional counselor or physician immediately.
2. If someone you trust urges you to seek counseling, schedule a session with a professionally trained counselor to evaluate your condition.
3. If you experience persistent and prolonged changes in sleep patterns, or if you experience a significant change in weight (either gain or loss), consult your physician.
4. If you are plagued by consistent, prolonged, severe feelings of hopelessness, consult a physician, a professional counselor, or your pastor.

In the familiar words of John 10:10, Jesus promises, "I have come that they may have life, and that they may have it more abundantly" (NKJV). And in John 15:11, He states, "These things I have spoken to you, that My joy may remain in you, and that your joy may be full." These two passages make it clear: our Savior intends that we experience lives of joyful abundance through Him. Our duty, as grateful believers, is to do everything we can to receive the joy and abundance that can be ours in Christ—and the term "everything" includes appropriate medical treatment when necessary.

Some days are light and happy, and some days are not. When we face the inevitable dark days of life, we must choose how we will respond. Will we allow ourselves to sink even more deeply into our own sadness, or will we do the difficult work of pulling ourselves out? We bring light to the dark days of life by turning first to God, and then to trusted family members, to friends, and, in some cases, to medical professionals. When we do, the clouds will eventually part, and the sun will shine once more upon our souls.

If you or someone you know seems to be dangerously sad, don't sit around and wait for things to get better. Get help ASAP.

Don't Focus on Appearances

Man does not see what the Lord sees,
for man sees what is visible, but the Lord sees the heart.
1 Samuel 16:7 Holman CSB

It's downright stressful to "keep up appearances." And besides, it's fruitless. After all, the world sees you as you appear to be, but God sees you as you really are—He sees your heart, and He understands your intentions. The opinions of others should be relatively unimportant to you; however, God's view of you—His understanding of your actions, your thoughts, and your motivations—should be vitally important.

Few things in life are more futile than keeping up appearances for the sake of neighbors. What is important, of course, is pleasing your Father in heaven while you provide support and encouragement to your family members and your closest friends.

Today, do yourself a favor: worry less about physical appearances and more about spiritual realities. It's the wise way—and the peaceful way—to live.

If you find yourself focusing too much on your appearance, it's time to find a different focus. Remember that God sees you as you really are, and it's God's view that matters.

If the narrative of the Scriptures teaches us anything, from the serpent in the Garden to the carpenter in Nazareth, it teaches us that things are rarely what they seem, that we shouldn't be fooled by appearances.

John Eldredge

Outside appearances, things like the clothes you wear or the car you drive, are important to other people but totally unimportant to God. Trust God.

Marie T. Freeman

Stress and Addiction

Do not have other gods besides Me.
Exodus 20:3 Holman CSB

If you'd like a perfect formula for creating stress, here it is: become addicted to something that destroys your health or your sanity. If (God forbid) you allow yourself to become addicted, you're steering straight for a boatload of negative consequences, not to mention a big bad dose of negative self-esteem.

Ours is a society that glamorizes the use of drugs, alcohol, cigarettes, and other addictive substances. Why? The answer can be summed up in one word: money. Simply put, addictive substances are big money makers, so suppliers (of both legal and illegal substances) work overtime to make certain that people like you sample their products. The suppliers need a steady stream of new customers because the old ones are dying off (fast), so they engage in a no-holds-barred struggle to find new users—or more accurately, new abusers.

The dictionary defines *addiction* as "the compulsive need for a habit-forming substance; the condition of being habitually and compulsively occupied with something." That definition is accurate, but incomplete. For Christians, addiction has an additional meaning: it means compulsively worshipping something other than God.

Unless you're living on a deserted island, you know people who are full-blown addicts—probably lots of people. If you, or someone you love, is suffering from the blight of addiction, remember this: Help is available. Plenty of people have experienced addiction and lived to tell about it . . . so don't give up hope.

And if you're one of those fortunate people who hasn't started experimenting with addictive substances, congratulations! You have just spared yourself a lifetime of headaches and heartaches.

Managing Money Wisely

Good planning and hard work lead to prosperity,
but hasty shortcuts lead to poverty.
Proverbs 21:5 NLT

If you're plagued by stress-inducing financial troubles, you're not alone. You inhabit a world where financial stress is rampant. And how can you resolve the stress of managing money wisely? Oftentimes, it's simply a matter of spending less.

Living on a budget sounds so easy, but it can be so hard. After all, we live in a world that is filled to the brim with wonderful things to buy and wonderful people telling us that we need to buy those things. But sometimes, our desires for more and better stuff can overload our ability to pay for the things we want. That's when Old Man Trouble arrives at the door.

The answer to the problem of overspending is straightforward. What's required is discipline. First, we must earn money through honest work for which we are well suited; then, we must spend less than we earn (and save the rest intelligently). This strategy of earning and saving money is simple to understand but much harder to put into practice.

Thankfully, God has clear instructions that, when followed, can lead us on the proper path.

God's Word reminds us again and again that our Creator expects us to lead disciplined lives. God doesn't reward laziness, misbehavior, or apathy. To the contrary, He expects us to behave with dignity and discipline. But ours is a world in which dignity and discipline are often in short supply.

When we pause to consider how much work needs to be done, we realize that self-discipline is not simply a proven way to get ahead, it's also an integral part of God's plan for our lives. If we genuinely seek to be faithful stewards of our time, our talents, and our resources, we must adopt a disciplined approach to life. There's simply no other way.

Here's a recipe for handling money wisely: Take a heaping helping of common sense, add a sizeable portion of self-discipline, and mix with prayer.

Marie T. Freeman

If you work hard and maintain an attitude of gratitude, you'll find it easier to manage your finances every day.

John Maxwell

When People Behave Badly

Don't answer a fool according to his foolishness,
or you'll be like him yourself.
Proverbs 26:4 Holman CSB

All of us can be grumpy, hardheaded, and difficult to deal with at times. And all of us, from time to time, encounter folks who behave in the same way, or worse. If you have occasion to deal with stress-inducing people (and you will), the following tips should help:

1. Do Make Sure That You're Not the One Being Difficult: Perhaps the problems that concern you have their origin, at least partially, within your own heart. If so, fix yourself first (Philippians 2:3).

2. Don't Try to Change the Other Person: Unless the person you're trying to change is a young child, and unless you are that child's parent or guardian, don't try to change him or her. Why? Because teenagers and adults change when they want to, not when you want them to (Proverbs 10:14).

3. Don't Lecture: Lectures inevitably devolve into nagging; nagging creates animosity, not lasting change. Since nagging usually creates more problems than it solves, save your breath (Proverbs 15:1).

4. Do Insist Upon Logical Consequences to Irresponsible Behavior: When you protect other people from the consequences of their misbehavior, you're doing those folks a profound disservice. Most people don't learn new behaviors until the old behaviors stop working, so don't be an enabler (Hebrews 12:5-6).

5. Don't Allow Yourself to Become Caught Up in the Other Person's Emotional Outbursts: If someone is ranting, raving, or worse, you have the right to get up and leave. Remember: emotions are highly contagious, so if the other person is angry, you will soon become angry, too. Instead of adding your own emotional energy to the outburst, you should make the conscious effort to remain calm—and part of remaining calm may be leaving the scene of the argument (Proverbs 22:24-25).

6. Do Stand Up for Yourself: If you're being mistreated, either physically, emotionally, or professionally, it's time to start taking care of yourself. But remember that standing up for yourself doesn't require an angry outburst on your part; you can (and probably should) stand up for yourself in a calm, mature, resolute manner. And you should do so sooner rather than later (Psalm 27:1).

7. Do Forgive: If you can't find it in your heart to forgive those who have hurt you, you're hurting yourself more than you're hurting anyone else. But remember: forgiveness should not be confused with enabling. Even after you've forgiven the difficult person in your life, you are not

compelled to accept continued mistreatment from him or her (Matthew 6:14-15).

8. Do Learn to Laugh at the Absurdities of Life: Life has a lighter side—look for it, especially when times are tough. Laughter is medicine for the soul, so take your medicine early and often (Proverbs 17:22).

9. Do Accept Personal Responsibility for Making Your Own Corner of the World Peaceful, Productive, Purposeful, and Palatable: If your world is a little crazy, perhaps it's time to consult the woman you see in the mirror. With God's help, you can discover a peace that passes understanding (Philippians 4:7-8). And if you genuinely work to bring peace into your own life (and into the lives of your loved ones) you will be rewarded (1 Corinthians 3:8, 13).

We are all fallen creatures and all very hard to live with.

C. S. Lewis

Bear with the faults of others as you would have them bear with yours.

Phillips Brooks

Finding and Sharing Encouragement

But encourage each other daily, while it is still called today,
so that none of you is hardened by sin's deception.
Hebrews 3:13 Holman CSB

Life is a team sport, and all of us need occasional pats on the back from our teammates. This world can be a difficult place, a place where many of our friends and family members are troubled by the stresses and challenges of everyday life. And since we cannot always be certain who needs our help, we should strive to speak helpful words to all who cross our paths.

In his letter to the Ephesians, Paul writes, "Do not let any unwholesome talk come out of your mouths, but only what is helpful for building others up according to their needs, that it may benefit those who listen" (4:29 NIV). This passage reminds us that, as Christians, we are instructed to choose our words carefully so as to build others up through wholesome, honest encouragement. How can we build others up? By celebrating their victories and their accomplishments. As the old saying goes, "When someone does something good, applaud—you'll make two people happy."

Genuine encouragement should never be confused with pity. God intends for His children to lead lives of abundance, joy, celebration and praise—not lives of self-pity or regret. So we must guard ourselves against hosting (or joining) the "pity parties" that so often accompany difficult times. Instead, we must encourage each other to have faith—first in God and His only begotten Son—and then in our own abilities to use the talents God has given us for the furtherance of His kingdom and for the betterment of our own lives.

As a faithful follower of Jesus, you have every reason to be hopeful, and you have every reason to share your hopes with others. When you do, you will discover that hope, like other human emotions, is contagious. So do the world (and yourself) a favor: Look for the good in others and celebrate the good that you find. When you do, you'll be a powerful force of encouragement to your friends and family . . . and a worthy servant to your God.

No journey is complete that does not lead through some dark valleys. We can properly comfort others only with the comfort we ourselves have been given by God.

Vance Havner

A SUMMARY: 17 ESSENTIAL STRESS-BUSTING TIPS

1. In Managing Stress, Make Sure That God Is Your Partner: God is big enough and strong enough to solve any problem you will ever face, so lean on Him.

2. Pray Early and Often: If you're experiencing too much stress, you should make sure that you're not neglecting your prayer life. Prayer is a powerful tool for managing stress: use it.

3. Get Enough Rest: Exhaustion is God's way of telling you to slow down. You need rest, and it's up to you (and only you) to make sure you get it.

4. Set Priorities Carefully: Since you can't do everything, you should make sure that your priorities are appropriate to your circumstances and pleasing to God.

5. Guard Your Thoughts: Since your thoughts have the power to magnify stress or decrease it dramatically, you should monitor the quality, the direction, and the veracity of those thoughts.

6. Don't Neglect Your Daily Devotional: If you're serious about beating stress, form the habit of talking to God first thing every morning.

7. Defeat Procrastination: Procrastination increases stress; intelligent action decreases it. Act accordingly.

8. Don't Engage in Needless Self-Criticism: If you become your own worst critic, you're creating needless stress for yourself and your loved ones.

9. Learn to Say No: When your calendar is full, you should learn to say "No" politely, firmly, and as often as necessary.

10. Learn to Conquer Those Everyday Frustrations: Angry thoughts are stress-inducing thoughts. So if you want to defeat stress, you must learn to control your temper before your temper controls you.

11. Don't Let Those Temporary Setbacks Get You Down: Don't hit the panic button, don't overreact, and don't give up. And remember that genuine success depends upon your relationship with God and His only begotten Son. Period.

12. Don't Worry About Keeping Up with the Joneses: Peer pressure can be very stressful. So you must focus more about pleasing God and less about pleasing your neighbors.

13. Seek God's Guidance: If you'd like a prescription for relieving stress—or for solving any other problem—ask God.

14. Learn to Trust God More and Worry Less: Needless worry creates needless stress. So when you're troubled, turn your concerns over to God and leave them there.

15. Work Hard and Leave the Rest to God: Do your best and trust God with the rest. And that means accepting the things you cannot change.

16. Praise God Every Day: Want to overcome the stresses of everyday life? Try spending more time thanking God and praising Him for His blessings.

17. Celebrate Life: "This is the day the Lord has made; let us rejoice and be glad in it." (Psalm 118:24 Holman CSB)